I0151094

And I Said No!

The Selling Of A Soul Brother To A Beer Company

James Hobson Jr.

Milligan Books   **California**

Published and Distributed by:
Milligan Books, Inc.

Cover Design
Paula N. White Designs

Book Design/Formatting
Alpha Desktop Publishing

First Printing, 1993
Second Printing, June 2003
1098765432

ISBN 0-9742811-1-5

The following literary work is a non-fiction account based on a true story. The names and identities of certain parties have been altered to either protect their innocence or obscure their guilt according to their involvement.

Milligan Books, Inc.
1425 W. Manchester Ave., Suite C
Los Angeles, California 90047
www.milliganbooks.com
drrosie@aol.com
(323) 750-3592

Dedication

Dedicated To

Jimmy Brewton

A.K.A.

Jimmy B.–J.B.

One of the unsung heroes of the movement.

A soldier whose heart, intellect and

insight surpassed the few short years

we had him in this world.

Contents

FOREWORD

MOTIVATION FOR WRITING THIS BOOK

For many years, I have walked around with this over-whelming sense of guilt. I have been looked upon by my co-workers, my peers, and members of my wife's family (now ex-family) as being less than a responsible person, husband and employee. I feel that I've been victimized. I was put in a precarious, untenable position that was destined for failure.

As I reflect over it, this large National Beer Company carefully orchestrated a plan for my demise. They didn't know exactly when I would fall out of the system, but they knew with all of the psychological and work pressures, all the underhandedness, that I would certainly fall from grace. So, I wrote this book—first to tell the story, and second because I'd hate to see another minority person experience this horrible fate. The climate in America has changed. Affirmative action is suspect these days. So, I think there's a high probability that these types of retaliatory actions will be more prevalent in the corporate world.

I have been a reluctant participant in a number of these corrupt corporate actions against other employees at "The Company"—planning, organizing, and systematically orchestrating the demise of other people. Therefore, I know first hand that it happened. It happened to them; it happened to me!

The company's methods were haphazard. They never really stopped to cover all of their bases; to really make their accusations against me foolproof. There were holes in their allegations. The company executives would contradict each other in their stories. So, there is no question in my mind that all of this was planned, orchestrated, and carried out. My career and personal life were methodically dismantled with the meticulous precision of a military strategist.

I guess, like a lot of young people, I started out in my career being very optimistic, energetic, and I thought that all you had to do was work hard, be honest and the world would be your oyster. However, after all of the manipulations I endured, I found out that it's not quite that way. You have to be cunning and devious to be successful in corporate America. Always watching and being mindful of what's going on around you. The corporate culture or, should I say, corporate jungle!

The loss of my job really hurt, but I guess my pride was hurt more than anything else. It wasn't the title or money that counted. It was the image I no longer held, the self-esteem that I no longer possessed.

INTRODUCTION

Blowing The Whistle For Public Awareness

During the Clarence Thomas Supreme Court hearings in October, 1991, many people wondered, "Why didn't Anita Hill come forward sooner?" A lot of times I reflect over the events that have transpired over the seven years that I worked for "The Company." As I reflect upon them now, I think at some point, I should have raised the flag or said, "enough is enough," or left The Company. If I had left The Company then, at least I could have gone without a job for a while. However, it's tough to explain to a potential employer why you're not employed, no matter the reason. But I stuck it out and stuck it out. I was afraid to blow the whistle for fear of reprisal.

For speaking out, if they didn't fire me, I would never have been promoted. Or, I would have been promoted to a locality that was even worse than my present one. I believe, at some point in time, my uncensored candor would have all caught up with me. There's no question in my mind about that. I would have risked being permanently blacklisted from corporate employment in America.

I first developed the fear of reprisal after the Leo Sampson incidents. Leo Sampson and Titus Marlowe were two Blacks that worked together in Ohio. Titus was a District Manager and Leo, an Area Manager. But when Leo wrote a letter regarding my boss Bruno's "Hitler" tactics, he was subsequently transferred to a region that had a higher cost of living. Leo had a large family, and that was an enormous strain on him. There were no company restraints on Bruno Pittman's behavior in the Ohio Division. His sentiments and actions were completely tolerated by The Company.

Bruno Pittman was the Division Manager who controlled the fate of all "The Company's" sales and marketing employees in Ohio. Leo Sampson was "The Company's" Area Manager in Ohio, responsible for the "Black" markets in the state. He was subsequently transferred to the east coast by Bruno, and shortly thereafter, left The Company.

I want people to be aware that companies in America will manipulate you, they will promote you for appearances. This often is a public relations ploy to project an image as an equal opportunity employer (often to take advantage of federal tax credits). Many women are victimized, too. The victims don't always know it, particularly single mothers, young college graduates, Blacks, minorities and females. They don't start out equal. They're not perceived as being equal. It's not planned for you to be on the same track as your white male counterparts. They have decided how far you're going to go and that's it! The glass ceiling for this group is made of cast iron.

This ceiling does exist. If you don't go along with the corruption, if you don't play the game by their rules, then you're ostracized. All of your years of education and sacrifice, all of the hard work, your future plans and career dreams, will be shattered. Either you play ball by their rules on their field, with their ball, or you perish.

I know this is a very disturbing message for the public to hear. We all would prefer not to think there's corruption in our major corporations. But I wish I could say that there is a light at the end of the tunnel. I think this book may be the light. I hope it will raise the public's awareness of what's really happening on your job. Many of the people you interface with on a daily basis are driven by corruption and you are merely an instrument of their manipulations.

The Company, Inc., and other corporations could be more sensitive to women and minority issues, and so could the white managers they assign as supervisors over minority subordinates. They need to be more cognizant of what's going on in their field offices. These supervisors should be in the company headquarters, where the company president can just look out of his office window or down the hall and see what's going on. They should see what's happening in these remote operations when you put these people in charge, how they are handling the authority they were given.

I hope this book will help stop the perpetuation of this phenomenon. If you immediately say no, if you refuse to participate, if you let them know at the outset that you cannot be manipulated, you cannot be intimidated, then that's good! Reassure yourself, if you have to sacrifice your employment, then sacrifice it with your head held high, not leaving the company in disgrace down the road.

The disgrace scenario is what happened to me. I was always wondering, who knew? I once applied for a job that I didn't get. I wondered why didn't I get it? Was it because I wasn't qualified or was it because they knew the reason I was fired?

I was perennially worried if I had been blacklisted. It's like you're dealing with some mega infrastructure. When you've been fired by one major company, it can keep the doors closed for you with others. Nevertheless, it's still ethically correct to retain your personal integrity and not sell out for material gain or employment security.

Over these past years, I've had to resign myself to the reality that I was no longer deemed employable by a Fortune 500 company. As a consequence, I've had to take a lesser job and adjust to working with less sophisticated employees.

My wife's family, a prominent Black family in the midwest, found out about my termination, but I never told any members of my own family. So, I have no idea what they know or what they may be afraid to confront me about. This fact is emotionally agonizing and something that I always think about. Their first exposure to my own story regarding the loss of my job (something that has been a mystery until now) will come from reading this book. I obsess endlessly about being placed in another corporate work setting and being manipulated the same way. For example, to be told I have to fire an employee that really should not be fired. Or to manipulate an employee as a means to achieve some devious corporate end. I don't want to be responsible for any duties except those in the job description. I've become overly cautious of my relationships with women. Now with a woman, I wonder what her hidden motives might be. Does she have a hidden agenda? I wonder what repercussions may come from my actions, as innocent as I may think they are.

I've carried this book in the back of my mind for years. I've known that The Company is a formidable opponent, a major entity. I was intimidated because of possible reprisals by the corporation. I've been reluctant to have a real close personal relationship, reluctant to be married, reluctant to have a family for fear of what might happen as a result of this book.

My life has been in a perpetual holding pattern, an emotional prison, tormented by my inexorable obsession to vindicate my name and warn the public.

I'm now prepared for the consequences. And the worse thing that could happen is that I could be charged with a crime, labeled a rapist, or even assassinated. But if that should be my fate, then it will be better than being among the living dead. My life was ruined and this is my only salvation. If I must be a martyr for my beliefs, then so be it.

I may be setup and charged with a criminal offense. Simply driving down the street, the police could pull me over, harass me and charge me with bogus charges.

Certainly I'd like to be as idealistic as anyone about corporate life in America. I'm as skeptical as the next guy about unusual things brought up to discredit major corporations. But this story is true. I have seen and experienced it first hand. And my conscience won't let me rest. Sometimes you have to stand up for something. There are times that you have to throw caution to the wind and say, "Yeah, what have I got to lose?" But on the other side of the coin, what is there to gain? And maybe a lot of people are going to say, "Yeah, he was a conformist, or he should have been more responsible."

Those views certainly concern me, but there is another group of people out there, the people who are more like me who are going to say, "Thank God someone blew the whistle." Maybe it might change things. Maybe it will help somebody. I have little to gain other than emotional exoneration. But who's going to be the one person to stand up and say, "Well, you're exonerated, Jim." Ultimately, my absolution will come from myself. I'm taking a stand to tell a story I feel compelled to tell, despite the possible embarrassment or reprisals.

One of my deepest regrets is the loss of my wife. I had a meeting with her about a year ago. I should have done that ten years ago and explained everything to her, instead of keeping everything locked up inside me, but I was so hurt and ashamed.

Instead of keeping things inside, I should have explained my experience to my wife in meticulous detail. I didn't before, but I did a year ago. Oddly enough, after all this time, she somewhat understood. One indelible phrase she said to me was: "This stinks to high heaven." And when I was able to relate my feelings, at critical points in time, she said, "Oh, that's why… I thought I sensed something, but I didn't know what it was and you weren't talkative, you didn't want to talk about it." I'm doing this not so much to ask for her forgiveness. Although, unquestionably, I want that because I respect her and love her. But this book is another way for me to apologize to my wife, to say, "I'm sorry. This is why it happened."

The Awakening

1

Sobering in The Jail Cell

Alone with my racing thoughts, in the obscurity of a dingy jail cell, I stood, trembling with fear on the cold, wet cement floor. As I stared into space, slowly my eyes began to catch a glimpse of daylight creeping through the barred window across the passageway from my cell door. It seemed with each ray of sunlight came a piercing clarity of perception about the sequence of events leading to this predicament. How could this have happened? How could life be filled with such paradoxes? Corporate executive one minute, humiliated and carrying the stigma of a criminal the next. Where did things go wrong? Who was to blame for this?

I was arrested about midnight, November 1984, with my friend and co-worker, Sean, and two company associates. By the time we were booked for "rape" and finally put into a jail cell, we had been moved around a lot. We were moved from a holding section to a cell with 30 to 40 other people. We had been in that cell for about an hour, and then, I guess because of our positions at The Company, we were moved to a cell with just ourselves.

That was the first time I had an opportunity to be alone with my thoughts. I was not being questioned or looking curiously at the other people around me. As I redirected my focus, I began to reflect upon what was actually happening, sobering up to the realities of my plight, and wondering how I got there.

I was slightly intoxicated when I was arrested. But by the time we were taken to the cell, I was sober. A sobriety that left me longing for a stiff drink to take me away from a reality that now had become a nightmare.

Once before, I had been arrested when I was 16 years old. I think the police put me in the jail cell then to scare me more than anything else. But I always knew I was getting out, I knew my mother was coming to pick me up. I knew it was just a matter of minutes, so I really wasn't too concerned.

This is what happened. I was standing in line to go to a high school championship basketball game. I was shoving, like everyone else, and a policeman came by and began hitting everyone on the leg with his nightstick. He told us, "Don't shove, straighten up, or go to the back." He hit me on the chin, and I yelled something that really made him mad. He yanked me out of the line and said, "You can't go into the basketball game."

Well, it was a championship game, and I got in anyway. I had an admission ticket, but I went against his wishes. He saw me at half time at the concession stand, and he grabbed me by the back of my neck, twisted my arm behind my back as if I had murdered someone, and hauled me off, threw me in the back of a police car and took me to jail. Of course, that was Chicago, it was the sixties, and over-exuberant policemen were well known for their violent potential, particularly with Blacks. I was just 16. I could not be charged as an adult, but my driver's license said that I was 17. The policemen seized that opportunity and put me in an adult cell with a gentleman who said he was there for *"murder."*

But that didn't affect me because I knew my mother was coming. And she did come about two hours later, paying $25 bail for my release. I went to court a few weeks later. The judge dismissed the case. So that was the extent of my encounters with the law up until this incident.

I was arrested in the middle of November in St. Louis, MO., so it was indeed cold outside. Since everything but the floor was metal—metal walls, cement floors and metal bars—it was cold inside too. I was never fingerprinted. They never took a mug shot. From the detective's room, we were escorted to the large cell with other people. I was handcuffed to Sean, and Peter's hands were handcuffed together.

We were escorted into a large cell with many other individuals. There were about 30 to 40 people in the cell; most of them were Black. Before that, we went to the area where you had to give up your personal belongings. People in the other cell could see what was going on. And I remember thinking, wow, I wish I didn't have this camel hair jacket on because if I'm going to be in this environment, I want to blend in, not look like some Corporate America person walking into this cell, with two white boys.

In the cell with all these strange people, the two white guys were exceptionally nervous. So was I. But you could see fear on their faces. They pulled out their cigarettes and began to smoke nervously. All the other prisoners in the cell just swooped down on them like vultures, saying, "Hey, can I have a cigarette?" And they were so nervous that they gave all of their cigarettes away. They were lucky they kept the cigarettes they lit up. That was it. The guys just took their cigarettes.

When we got to the holding cell, we were unhandcuffed. In the cell, there was no place to sit, no place to lie down or anything. I remember telling the two white guys that we had to hang tough. I was the guy that was comforting them, and I remember later when we were in the cell just the three of us, one of them asked me, "Have you been through this before?"

Maybe this was their first experience with anything even remotely similar to this. They were totally unglued, because these were upper middle class white boys now thrust into this situation.

In the holding cell were mostly uneducated skid row types and gangbangers, big guys with massive arms, muscular necks, guys that resembled stereotypical images of men incarcerated, with nothing else to do but work out with weights to discharge their anger.

There were haggard urban transients, dressed in old tattered clothes that smelled horrible. There were also younger toughs who wore what was then traditional habiliments: long coats, army coats and short jackets.

Their language was very, very gruff, they used a lot of profanity. In fact, 20 feet away was a cell with two or three women, and there was banter going back and forth about, "Baby, what I'd like to do to you." One girl was saying to one of the prisoners, "Well, I don't want you, I want the other

one ... and bring it on, daddy!" There were multiple conversations going back and forth. And they were really into it, I
guess a way to pass the time.

I may have seemed cool on the exterior, but if they could
have seen what was going on inside my head, they would have
said this guy is really shaken up.

I pondered, "What am I doing here? How did this
happen? Don't they know this charge is a lie? I'm going to be
out of here in a few minutes ... they can't be for real ...What if
seven o'clock arrives and I have to go to work? Are they going
to get their act together and let me go, so I can go back to the
hotel, clean up, shave and go to work?"

I couldn't believe this was continuing, that it was going
on without an abrupt end. I just knew that they were going to
come and tell us to go home, they'd made a mistake, and that
would be the end of it. I don't think I was cool because the
white boys perceived me as being tough, it was just because I
knew that if I showed any weakness or nervousness, that I
would be what's known as "jail bait," a guy who is susceptible
to being beat up in his cell.

I didn't have any valuables on me at the time. There I was
with these white boys and wearing a white button down shirt, a
camel hair jacket, and wing-tipped shoes. I figured my
appearance and my persona would make me the kind of prey
jail gangsters would want to come after and beat up.

I began looking around suspiciously, trying to put my
back against the wall for protection, and being very observant
of what was going on around me. I didn't want to have to look
over my back. I only wanted to look straight ahead. Being in a
cell with about 30 or 40 people, and having seen enough prison

movies and television shows, I knew my best approach for observing what was going on around me, was to try to get as close to the wall as possible. Also, it's easier leaning against the wall for an hour and a half, than just standing up.

I don't know where the jail was because the police transported us in a van. I presume it was the downtown main jail. But I don't presume it was the county jail. But I had no idea where I was, what part of the city I was in … I had no idea. Was I in the downtown lockup or in the County Jail or what? They had permitted me one telephone call before taking us to the holding cell, and I called a co-worker, Robert Gladstone, who said, "Well, okay Jim, you know I'll do something." But I had no idea what he was doing, or if he would rectify the situation, and I was hoping he wasn't going around telling everybody at The Company that I was in jail.

I was hoping he would be somewhat discreet, and could perform this miracle before I was due to show up to work the next morning. Even though I had been incarcerated before for an hour and a half, that was at a neighborhood police station, there was only one other person in the cell and it happened in the early afternoon. Also I wasn't hungry or tired or scared.

It had to be close to three or four o'clock in the morning. They had taken my watch, as part of my personal belongings, so I was also disoriented. I began to realize that Sean and I were not going to make it to work on time—if at all. I also was worrying about how this rape allegation was going to affect my job and my marriage.

They finally took me and the other two guys to an elevator and put us in a smaller cell. The window was the frosted type that you couldn't see in or out. But I could tell that daylight was coming.

Daylight outside, and I could feel the cold because there was poor ventilation. It was icy cold. At that time, it must have been about 4:30 - 5:00 a.m.

In the cell, the three of us had individual metal fold-out beds on metal slates. At least we could lie down. That's when I really had the chance to focus away from self-protection and onto what was really happening here.

Then it started sinking in with me that I was in St. Louis. St. Louis lies along the Mississippi, and is known as the "Gateway City." Depending on your perspective it could be a gateway to the North or the South. Proximity would perhaps lend St. Louis to the North, but in racial attitude, tradition and ethnic sensitivity, well, welcome to Dixie! Now, I thought, I'm really in for an emotional roller coaster ride. The alleged rape victim was white, and I was a Black man. And this is happening in a city with Southern attitudes. In the past, they hung "niggers" for just whistling at or looking at white women in the South.

I had read enough books, seen enough movies to know that I could quite possibly be in some very serious trouble here. Could I even be facing the death penalty? I looked over at the two white guys on the other cot. Once in awhile we would talk to one another. Suddenly, the tables turned, it seemed to me that they were composed and I was fearing the reality of my predicament as a Black man. I was starting to become more emotionally unglued.

Now I was wondering would they turn state's evidence against me, and go scott free. I'd be the scapegoat, the one carrying the weight for all of this. So, that was going on in my mind. Since I said "no" to testifying against Titus Marlowe, and participated in some things that were either illegal or immoral against other employees of The Company, I started wondering if this wasn't all "a setup," too.

And I said no! For my refusal to testify, would this be the retribution? Was this whole situation contrived? I had been involved in and witnessed so many employee setups that now I wondered if I wasn't a victim of a corporate setup myself. A well-devised corporate conspiracy that strikes employees with the lethal blow of a King Cobra. I thought about loopholes in the law, and based on what I had read and seen on television, how one defendant can "turn state's evidence" against his co-defendant.

I again looked at my cellmates. Was this part of a master plan orchestrated by The Company, Inc.? My thoughts drifted back to my first interview with Bruno, the uneasiness I felt on the airplane ride home to Chicago after my interview. Then my meeting with Charles Foster and Leo Sampson in San Francisco when they told me I worked for "Little Hitler." I thought about how the Jewish wholesaler, Michael Goldberg, was setup and what happened to Helen Barken. Bruno's drive-by with Steve Lyons, my secret meeting with the Regional Manager in South Bend, Indiana, my surprise meeting with the attorneys in Bruno's office. Was this just another event in the episode of my employment? My mind became a human rolodex of mental activity.

My elbow was on the ledge of the cell door as I looked out into the frosted window, wondering if I could end up in a penitentiary, in a state where I had no friends. Far away from home. Far away from everyone that I knew and loved. How vulnerable I felt. I was not in my home state where I grew up. I had no clout, and my mother was not coming to bail me out!

About this time, the jailer unlocked the cell door and, without a word, led us to a very small dimly lit room the size of a small closet and locked the three of us in it. On the side of a wire-mesh window was an attorney friend of Robert Gladstone's; Robert had come through. The attorney, in a very low tone, asked if we had made any statements, we told him no, he replied not to, and he would get us released that day. A few minutes passed and the jailer unlocked the door and led us back to our cell. This was my only contact with the outside world; it was comforting knowing that a professional was on the outside working on my behalf. At least, I could finally look forward to being released, getting a shower and something to eat. There was still the moral dilemma; what were we going to tell the managers at the brewery regarding why we were late, and didn't call? I trusted that somehow Robert would take care of it.

An hour or two later, the jailer returned. He led us to the elevator and then to the window where we had deposited our valuables. This period seemed like an eternity. I didn't even bother to count the money in my wallet, I just wanted to get the hell out of that place. We passed through a couple of doors and then were greeted by our attorney's young assistant. We sat on a bench as he explained that we were being released on our own recognizance and, pending some decision, might have to return to St. Louis. He then drove us to our hotel.

When I got to my hotel room, the message light was flashing on the telephone. It was a message from Dan Dezenso,

Vice President of the Sales Division of The Company. He requested that I meet him in the lobby of the St. Louis Convention Center. Oh well, he must have found out, I thought, but I hadn't done anything illegal. If I could get fired for poor moral judgment under the influence of Bratbrau, then company officers would have to fire a lot of the field marketing staff at The Company, I thought.

It was still before noon. I ordered room service and took a long hot shower. I tried to wash away the humiliation, shame and degradation from my prison experience. Sean and I took a cab to the convention center where Dan had his assistant, Vince Kelly, met us. Vince gave Sean and me separate envelopes. The letters inside said from this moment on, we were not to conduct any business on behalf of The Company until further notice.

Vince proceeded to explain that one of the police officials had called Hirsh H. Heidenthal, CEO of The Company, personally and informed him of our case. To make his point, Hirsh called all of the managers in town for the convention to an emergency meeting and told them of our indiscretions. Hirsh was extremely feared throughout the company. He was a no-nonsense, very intimidating manager with an icy stare.

One of the corporate jokes about Hirsh was that "if he ever smiled, his face would crack!" Bruno disliked Hirsh, and his nickname for him was "3 sticks." Bruno would often say discouraging things about Hirsh and the Heidenthal family, they were the brunt of many jokes. A book written by prize-winning journalists in St. Louis pointed out that in 1976, a member of the Hirsh family pleaded guilty to manslaughter.

Another son was reported to have bitten off an opponent's ear during a barroom brawl. But his favorite joke was about the CEO, who did not have a college education, whose wife allegedly left him for a much older St. Louis baseball announcer who had to move to announce baseball in Chicago.

Corporate Corruption: How It All Started

2

O ver the years, the biggest complaint I've heard from minority college graduates is that their institution of higher learning failed to teach them how to get ahead, "how to play the game," particularly in a corporation. Of course, there are many books available for outside reading such as: "Swimming in the Mainstream," by two Black employees at Xerox, and "What They Didn't Teach You at Harvard Business School."

For me, and for a lot of Blacks and minorities of my generation, we thought in order to "make it," all you had to do was be honest, hard working, and have a little luck. Of course, it's been postulated that the best education in the business world is the "school of hard knocks." It is in this corporate climate that the survival skills, e.g., cunning, deviousness, treachery and revenge, are typically introduced and nurtured. It is these unscrupulous practices that have prompted this book.

The golden opportunity, the chance of a lifetime, were resonating thoughts encouraged by my uncle who worked as a Schlitz beer salesman in Chicago. He constantly urged me to look to the brewing industry for employment before graduating from college. He felt that a Black with a bachelor's degree could make great strides in the early seventies. Maybe those pep talks influenced me to go to work for the Joseph Schlitz Brewing Company. At the time, it was the number two brewer in the world. I later learned that the company was embroiled in severe management problems, both in production and illegal marketing practices. After two years of waiting and hoping for Schlitz to turn around, now was my chance at the brass ring, the opportunity to work for The Company, Inc., the world's largest and the brewer of Bratbrau. It was 1978 and I was 27.

It took several interviews in Chicago with the Region Manager for the Mid-West, Richard Cline, and his assistants, before I was invited to interview for a position in Columbus as Area Manager for Ohio. I remember my initial thoughts of Columbus were that it was not a cosmopolitan city. But here was a possible opportunity to work for the world's largest brewers. I reasoned, with my ambition and determination, I wouldn't be there long anyway.

I flew to Columbus that Saturday for a meeting with the Ohio Division Manager, Bruno Pittman. Bruno and I met in the coffee shop at the Columbus Airport, and his interview was pretty much confined to my knowledge of the industry. Ironically, I learned that he was also from Chicago. After several cups of coffee, I was offered the job.

On the flight back, I had mixed emotions. I was happy about getting the position and the responsibility of 13 Black markets in Ohio. But it was hard to be excited about moving from Chicago to Columbus—and there was something about Bruno Pittman—something unsettling!

On June 17, 1978, after working out my two weeks notice with my present employer, I flew to Columbus that Sunday to start my employment with The Company. My home for the next month was the Inworth Hotel in Inworth, Ohio. A nice enough hotel stuck in the bedroom community of Inworth, with absolutely no attractions or distractions at all. This was a community that was not ethnically diverse. The next morning in the coffee shop, I was the only Black in the shop. This week was also my first exposure as a lonely resident in a community, and being without a car literally confined me to a hotel room.

Monday morning Bruno picked me up at the hotel and we proceeded to the division office. In those days, the staff was very small and the principal occupants were Bruno and his secretary Lynn Thaxton. Lynn was a single parent who had relocated to Columbus from a town in Texas. The first day was spent as usual in a new company, filling out numerous forms, neither Bruno nor Lynn were knowledgeable about the company's programs or benefits. Of course, this was not their area of expertise.

I was also issued company equipment: a work organizer, desktop calculator, typewriter and a cardboard box three feet high and three feet wide. The box haphazardly contained papers and notebooks that had belonged to my predecessor, Leo Sampson.

I recall asking, "Where is Leo now?" A question I should have asked before accepting the job. My question was ignored and I was advised by Bruno to study the contents of the box. In essence, that was my indoctrination and training program for my job at The Company.

Three District Managers constituted the rest of the marketing department in Ohio. Robert Gladstone, who resided in Cincinnati, was responsible for southern Ohio; Tom Johnson, who resided in Cleveland, had responsibilities for northeast Ohio; and the local District Manager, Ken Miller, who resided in Columbus, had responsibilities for central Ohio. On Thursday, I met Ken Miller and we proceeded to the local wholesaler of The Company products; the Central Distributing Company. After meeting all the employees and the owners of the company, Ken and I went to their conference room. It was policy for The Company Field Marketing people to utilize wholesalers'operations as offices. That morning, Ken went through the motions of instructing me how to fill out the weekly itineraries, expense account forms, and weekly market visit report.

Oddly, he would not let me see a completed form, only blanks. Ken also advised that these particular forms should be completed on weekends and that they were to be typed. At the time, each field sales manager was allotted fifteen dollars per day for trade calls. The trade call report form had lines only 1/8 inch wide for listing the appropriate information on three-sheet carbon paper.

Needless to say, I spent endless hours typing. One last item that my "mentor" told me was that I had to travel on my own time. That Friday, as I was about to depart from the division office en route to Chicago, Bruno advised that I had to take all the equipment, "box and all," with me and that I could not leave anything in the office. I was so concerned about the sensitive data in the cardboard box being lost or stolen. And so there I was, traveling each weekend, lugging my three-suiter, a briefcase, work organizer, portable typewriter, desktop calculator and a box large enough for a 32-inch television. Since no matter what city I worked in, I had to report to the division office in Columbus, Friday afternoons and Monday mornings, what would have been the harm leaving the equipment?

On my second plane ride from Columbus back to Chicago, I knew that there was something definitely wrong; a haunting feeling came over me, but I was determined that nothing was going to keep me from being a success at The Company. I was the first college graduate in my father's family, the second in my mother's, and I had to be a success; I had to be a source of pride and I also had to prove to myself that I could do the job. Honesty and integrity were the cornerstones of my work ethic; I figured I was a diamond in the rough and that eventually, senior management would know it.

The first month was exhausting; I had to leave home at 4 a.m. every Monday with all the equipment and boxes, and take two buses to O'Hare Airport in order to arrive at the division office by 8:30 a.m. It would be well after 9:00 p.m. by the time I got home on Fridays. Weekends were generally spent with Saturday-type activities, e.g. haircut, banking, cleaners, and of course, typing those 1/8 inch trade call reports and other reports on carbon paper.

After a month or so, Tom Johnson and Robert Gladstone came to Columbus for a few days. This was the first of what would become frequent after-hours drinking and partying until the early hours of the morning. Lynn would always get a couple of her girlfriends to join us and we would bar hop around northern Columbus. I had never been much of a drinker, and my partying had always been confined to the weekends. This was a new world—being the only Black and much younger than the other employees, I really felt isolated; I was constantly being urged to loosen up, let my hair down, to become part of the group. In many of the accounts and bars we frequented, I was the only minority.

A month had gone by when one day Bruno abruptly told me that I had to relocate to Columbus immediately. That to extend my stays in hotels in my home market would necessitate him having to fill out all matter of forms to the Vice President of Marketing, Douglas O'Donald. Yes, I was intimidated, I did not want to raise the eyebrows of a Vice President at the world headquarters, particularly after only one month of employment.

A few days later, I rented an apartment two blocks from the office. It wasn't what I preferred, but the rental office was accommodating enough to let me move in over the weekend. It was fortunate for me that my brother Larry was home from dental school for the summer. That weekend Larry, my brother Johnny, and I packed everything, rented a U-Haul truck, and moved me to Columbus. That Sunday evening, they took the Greyhound bus back to Chicago. Exhausted, I went to work that Monday morning.

The Company's District Managers and Area Managers are issued field marketing manuals. These manuals are designed to instruct the Field Manager on the how-to's of the various aspects of their jobs and employment. Such items as what forms to fill out and when, who and where to send them, relocating and the method for utilizing a moving carrier, all the topics that would have made my transition and acclimation a lot easier. I could not understand why my co-workers were so inhospitable—they offered no help in my relocation—and of course, all my personal business, e.g., phone service, utilities, postal service, had to be conducted on my lunch hour. It was a few months before I became aware of the manual's existence, and when I inquired as to when I would be issued a manual, I was advised by Bruno that the company had exhausted its supply and that I was the first on the list when they became available—yeah, right.

In early September, all the Field Managers from the midwest came to Chicago to write the Annual Market Plan. It was my first opportunity to meet the other managers, particularly the Blacks. The three other Blacks were: Mel Hunter, Area Manager for Illinois, Rick Gates, Area Manager for Michigan; and Donald Miles, District Manager in Detroit, Michigan. One evening, the Black guys took time to explain to me in detail that Bruno was an outright racist. They gave me the chilling account of how Bruno orchestrated the eventual firing of a Black District Manager, Titus Marlowe, in Columbus, Ohio, and the relocation and fall from grace of my predecessor Leo Sampson. I was told how Bruno wielded his power anyway he wanted, how he orchestrated devious plans and manipulated people to harass or victimize company employees at his discretion. Those he felt should be terminated from The Company were systematically harassed, made to give an impression of incompetence, and ultimately dismissed. Bruno did this without regard to employees' careers or families. And the people that he targeted most were subordinates that were Black and/or female. And, to make matters worse, The Company's senior management was insensitive and literally gave Bruno carte blanche. The Blacks had nicknamed Bruno, "Little Hitler," which was appropriate.

For the first time I came to grips with my emotions, everything that I had sensed, the unsettling feelings on the plane trips back to Chicago, the charade about the field marketing manual, the intimidation of moving myself to Columbus, the lack of training and orientation! My options were limited, Bruno was obviously part of the "good ole' boy network," and there was no higher authority to turn to. My only option was to quit—unthinkable! I did not come from a family of quitters. Once while in Army boot camp, I received a letter from my father in which he wrote, "I did it, so can you," and I had to draw upon those words one night in a foxhole 30 degrees below zero. And so, there it was, I would have to endure what generations had endured, it was just one more mountain to climb. Back in Columbus, Bruno picked an opportune time to ask if I had had an opportunity to talk to the other Blacks, as he was curious to know their sentiment towards him; my mind searched feverishly for a euphemistic response—to no avail. I could only respond, "Your name did not come up."

Charles Foster, the manager for Black Markets, was the highest ranking Black at The Company. Bruno was always quick to point out Charles' shortcomings; he would often say that he himself wasn't a racist but that Charles was pure window dressing. In September of 1978, I met Charles in Cincinnati for The Company's Sponsored Promotion.

I soon learned that Charles also had a dislike for Bruno; Charles reiterated what the other Blacks had said about Bruno and that until he became their boss, Titus Marlowe and Leo Sampson had had outstanding careers at The Company. I shall always remember the final words Charles spoke on the subject at breakfast in Cincinnati: "A leopard never ever changes his spots. Cover your ass."

That October, The Company held its Annual Convention in San Francisco, California. It was my first visit ever to California. I flew first class and stayed at the Hyatt Regency in Union Square; boy, was I hooked! The company was rebounding from a 99-day strike, which left consumers with no Bratbrau, and so they switched to Miller High Life; Miller Lite had also made a large in-road into the market. Industry analysts were writing and postulating that "It was not a matter of *if* Miller Brewing Company would surpass The Company, only *when!*"

The Company went all out for this convention, it wanted to display its image as the industry leader and build the morale of its employees and wholesalers before battle. There were approximately 950 Company wholesalers throughout the country, of which two were Black-owned. The Black-owned had sales areas in the poorest, bleakest crime ridden parts of the cities of Chicago and Los Angeles. You could say they were destined for failure. Wholesalers pick up beer from the breweries, house it in their warehouses, and sell the beer to retailers, e.g., baseball stadiums, bars, grocery stores, etc.

To become a wholesaler for a major brewer such as The Company, Miller Brewing Company, or Coors, meant a lot of money; I think it's safe to say you would be a millionaire. In those days, The Company would terminate wholesalers at the blink of an eye over a personality conflict, ethnicity, or religion.

I was overwhelmed with the convention, meeting so many people, the who's who of the industry. The restaurants, the entertainment, it was my exposure to everything I had ever imagined business would be.

Charles Foster's demeanor is that of a statesman. His years in public relations taught him to be retiring and charismatic, and he certainly knew how to look the part. Bruno Pittman and even the Blacks would comment on how Charles' office was the largest and nicest, second only to Douglas O'Donald, the Vice President of Marketing.

One afternoon when there was a planned break during the convention activities, Charles held a meeting in his suite for all the Blacks at the St. Regis Hotel (this is the hotel depicted as the St. Gregory in the evening television soap opera, "Hotel.") This was a time for a lot of firsts—my first time to meet the Blacks from the other parts of the country, and my first time in an elegant hotel suite.

There were about a dozen Blacks in Charles' suite, and this was my opportunity to meet my predecessor, Leo Sampson. The meeting was brief and every one left except for Charles, Leo and myself. Leo was a massive man, approximately six feet, five inches, 300 pounds. Physically a defensive linesman for anyone's football team, and he had to be intimidating to Bruno.

Conversely, his reports, which I read over and over again to try to learn and understand my job, gave me the insight that here was a man who was well read and of great intellect. In fact, I learned that Leo had previously worked for Davenport, Elliot, and Martin, The Company's advertising agency of record. I suspected that there would be little tolerance there for someone who couldn't perform, and obviously The Company knew his credentials before he was hired. We sat around the coffee table in Charles' suite and once again I began to hear this now familiar tale. Titus Marlowe was a graduate of Western Michigan University, a member of Kappa Alpha Psi Fraternity, an employee of The Company since 1962, a family man.

Titus was perhaps the third Black District Manager the company had ever had; he had been promoted numerous times over his fifteen-year tenure; his ability and dedication were well-documented. However, he was fired, June 13,1977. Charles and Leo began to tell me just how Bruno orchestrated Titus Marlowe's demise. Leo told me how the company was insensitive to Blacks and their plight. He produced a four-page memo that he had written to Bruno on November 20, 1977. Copied on the letter were Hirsh H. Heidenthal, Chief Executive Officer; Lantz L. Stone, President; J. R. Staggerman, Legal

Counsel; W. R. Teller, Vice President of Sales. Leo's memo accused Bruno of having a "Hitlerian disposition," of accusing Leo of a feeling of "special treatment," to misrepresenting of facts to The Company management.

[redacted]

[redacted]

[redacted]

Sir, while I sincerely regret the need for this Particular Kind of communication
to you I feel it is essential to our relationship and to my career with [redacted]
[redacted]

As I indicated in our telephone conversation of November 19, 1977, which, for your
information, was made with my own nickle, I thoroughly resent the insinuative and
insulting tone of the hereto attached communications from you. And I suggest that
sarcasm and oversight on your part, in combination with Hitlerian disposition, do
nothing for improved communication between men of any levels. In the past I have
neglected to bring this trait of yours to your attention out of respect for the
office you hold and in the interest of improving communications between us with or
ithout your stir. However, the influence of your office is not to be ignored, and
re importantly, your style of employing that influence from your level up is
clearly in need of our mutual superiors' attention. It has caused the termination
of one ▮ employee's fifteen-year career and now, for the <u>second</u> time in <u>one</u> year,
it threatens mine.

In short, you have forced me to speak out against you as I am not a blank page in
your coloring book which you may color as you please and then present to others as
a true picture of me.

In our phone conversation of November 19, 1977, you accused me of feeling that I
deserve "special treatment" -- for reasons you neglected to spell out and which I
do not understand -- and of continually sidestepping ▮▮ policy because of some
self-styled exemption from same. I deny both charges:

Your letter, copied to [redacted], shows no recognition of my having
informed you of the circumstances surrounding the missing receipts attach-
able to expense account for the week ending 11-5-77, which information I
imparted to you via my usual Monday morning phone call.

To refresh your memory, said call was made on Monday, November 7, 1977,
from Memphis, Tennessee. At that time I explained to you that I had
experienced car failure returning home from Columbus, Ohio on Friday, November 4, 1977, and that having to depart Cleveland again on Sunday, November 6, 1977, made it imperative that I use the current Saturday to effect
the necessary repairs. Since I had had to rent an automobile to complete
my trip home, and had not experienced this situation before, I explained
that I felt I should consult with you prior to completing my expense account. I discussed the matter with on Monday morning since previous attempts
to reach you had failed.

████████████████████████

████████████████████████

Additionally, I explained during that call that the ensuing incon-
veniences pertinent to the breakdown, two tow trips, one Friday and
one Saturday because of the time, contacts necessary for repairs
which were not completed until Sunday, and a hasty departure enroute
to Memphis had caused me to leave Cleveland not realizing that said
receipts were not in my possession. I did not inform you at that
time, because I did not know it, that I would not return to Cleveland
for two weeks, thus delaying submitting of the receipts even longer.

I fully realize that we all are sometimes faced with hectic and unscheduled in-
conveniences and I do not expect special treatment when they occur to me. Neither do I expect to be put on the defensive and misrepresented by you because of
such occurances. Your letter suggests that I left the receipts through sheer
carelessness.

As for your having to explain to ████████ about my missing receipts, I have no
idea that far more heinous offenses have been explained with less hooplah. I
ap... 'gize for the embarassment you seem to feel, but I am perfectly capable of
exp ining my own circumstances, to anyone, if and when you are ashamed of re-
laying my explanation as given to you.

You indicate also that I have submitted an expense report without receipts before;
When? How many times? How long ago? Your letter implies that this is a habi-
tual occurrence. Prove it. Again, your letter is an overreaction. It exagger-
ates -- to cover yourself -- and makes me appear a recalcitrant. People in this
company at many different levels, who have known me far longer than you, know that
this evaluation is not true of me. I thought I had proven that to you by now. I
have certainly made every effort to do so.

Further, you point out that I should be careful where I mail my weekly package to
you. I have made every effort to have my communications arrive in your office no
later than Tuesday of each week. When severly pressed and forced to mail late I
have sent the items special delivery. Any ridiculously late arrivals you seem to
have received have been due to the mails.

Pertinent to your reiteration of Division and/or Region Policy:

> 1. As pointed out, I rely heavily on Monday morning calls
> to provide you with correct information concerning my
> whereabouts. Again, we have discussed this before, it
> is not out of disregard that my route lists have not
> been mailed on Thursdays as you have suggested, and have
> instead been part of my weekend package. It is because
> it seems to me that misinformation is worse than no in-
> formation, especially when correct information will ar-
> rive timely enough -- via the Monday morning call.

Changes in time zones and the details of crew activity have
sometimes made it difficult to call before 9:30 a.m, but I
make every effort to do so.

2. Except under circumstances beyond my control, my mail has
been and will continue to be received by your office as
prescribed.

3. Failure to forward Market Visit Report for 10-31-77 was an
oversight on my part. I had not expected to be present at
Columbus post convention meetings, since I was not a participant, and the unexpected events of the ensuing weekend
allowed the one day in Brookpark, Ohio to slip my mind. I
will endeavor to be more observant in the future.

4. As my vacation had already been rescheduled once this year
and as I have not been certain of when it would actually
take place -- and as you and I discussed the subject at length
during our division meeting on Tuesday, November 1, 1977, and
its relevance to future crew activity -- vacation information
was sent to your office as soon as I could avoid providing
misinformation. You knew my plans via the aforementioned discussion and I observed you note the 11-21-77 date.

You indicate an absence of route lists for dates 11-14-77 and 10-3-77; Please
refer to route lists 9-24-77 and 10-1-77 for information concerning 10-3-77
and to route lists 11-5-77 and 11-12-77 for information concerning 11-14-77.

Finally, your note attached to my 11-4-77 Market Visit Report; " Is your
typewriter broken?" In my two years with ████████████ I have submitted
some 44 handwritten Market Visit Reports between Michigan and Ohio, more than
that when you add crew activity and convention, etc. I have done this because
I was informed, specifically, that it was not necessary to type the Market
Visit Report, only the Market Report (all of which I have typed). Why re-
proach me now about a handwritten and legible Market Visit Report? You have
not informed me of any change in division policy, yet, because of this report
you accuse me of disregarding same. Why?

In conclusion, while your disdain for me, personally, and for others in your
division, has occasionally been camouflaged by your professionalism, it has
reared its ugly head often enough not to be overlooked, at this point. As I
give you respect I expect respect from you in return. You have not recipro-
ted. While I do not claim to be perfect, neither do I intend to be labeled
irresponsible. In the past you have besmudged me professionally and impaired
my earning ability with ████████████ Continually, you have assaulted

page 4

my integrity and insulted my intelligence and caused others to be swayed by your inept and erroneous evaluations of me. I am not ashamed to admit that this letter takes the place of physical contact with you. For these reasons, I request a transfer from your division as soon as it can be arranged.

cc: Messrs.

The memo had also been circulated to many of the Blacks in marketing. The last paragraph, however, was echoed many times by the Black employees, and bears repeating here:

"In conclusion, while your disdain for me, personally, and for others in your division, has occasionally been camouflaged by your professionalism, it has reared its ugly head often enough not to be overlooked at this point. As I give you respect I expect respect from you in return. You have not reciprocated. While I do not claim to be perfect, neither do I intend to be labeled irresponsible. In the past you have besmudged me professionally and impaired my earning ability with The Company Inc. Continually, you have assaulted my integrity and insulted my intelligence and caused others to be swayed by your inept and erroneous evaluation of me. I am not ashamed to admit that this letter takes the place of physical contact with you. For these reasons, I request a transfer from your division as soon as it can be arranged."

Preis 40 Pfennig

Ploy to Eliminate Black Employees

3

A s if the "Hitlerism" indictment wasn't bad enough, Titus Marlowe had filed a racial discrimination suit against Bruno Pittman and The Company. I was told that this action was having a resounding effect because it not only affected The Company personnel, but also wholesalers personnel and ex-employees. People were subpoenaed for depositions, and certainly, what you said could affect your conscience or employment, and it most certainly was going to affect me.

Leo was transferred to New York, and The Company did not have a "cost of living adjustment" for people transferred to areas with higher cost. This was particularly tough for Leo; although his wife was a teacher, they had seven children; thus Leo had quite a commute from a Philadelphia suburb to New York. Finally, it was suggested that I contact Titus and his attorney, Scott Vaughn, for my own protection. I guess Leo's instincts, based on his and Marlowe's experience, knew that I was in for an experience for which I was totally unprepared.

So there I was, at a convention, in perhaps the prettiest city in the world, on a company expense account, in the most opulent room I had ever been in—being told by my predecessor that I was working for this "devil!"

When I arrived in San Francisco, I called a friend that I worked with at Schlitz Brewing Company in Chicago. Ron Nelson left Schlitz and through a close friend went to work for a major computer corporation in San Francisco. Over the weekend, I met Ron's friend, a Division Manager, and his wife Lisa. I guess they were kind of impressed with me and sort of intimated that I consider employment with their employer. Obviously, I didn't take the job (although now I wish I had) but the thought that I had friends in influential positions at a major corporation would be comforting on many occasions.

Dilemma Solution

The Company during this time was called the sleeping giant. But once confronted with a formidable opponent like Miller Brewing Company, policy began to change. New marketing employees had to have at least a bachelor's degree. The Division Managers for the midwestern region: Illinois; Iowa; Minnesota and Michigan had Master's Degrees.

So there it was; Titus Marlowe, Leo Sampson, and Charles Foster had degrees; all the field marketing managers in Ohio had degrees, except for Bruno Pittman. So all I had to do was not act too smart and not intimidate him like Titus and Leo must have done!

While in Columbus, Bruno instructed me to complete marketing reports for each of my thirteen markets. The report was very comprehensive and covered 100 categories of the wholesalers operation. The report was a legal document and could be integral in termination proceedings. My first bona fide verbal reprimand came as a result of my report for the Central Distributing Company. In my report, I stated that the 5-year business plan had not been completed. However, Ken Miller wrote in his market report earlier that year that the plan had been completed. I was chastised for not corroborating with Ken, and possibly causing embarrassment to the division office.

One day, around late October, Ken Miller, Robert Gladstone, Tom Johnson and I were in the conference room. Bruno took the opportunity to tell Tom Johnson and me of the course he wanted us to take with the Youngstown, Ohio wholesaler. He was a Jewish man named Michael Goldberg. Bruno stated that we should employ modern technology and put Michael Goldberg in a microwave oven!

I can remember being shocked, chills running through my body, totally dismayed. I thought I was going to vomit. As I looked at my co-workers, I could see the shock on their faces. In all honesty, I never heard a co-worker echo these sentiments. But Bruno would repeat this statement time after time. He also would include Charles Wadsworth, one of Michigan's largest wholesalers, who was also Jewish. Bruno then went on to say that we should delay requests for information i.e. budgets; building plans, and any reports due to heighten the chance of mistakes by the Wholesaler and thus put him in a precarious position with senior management.

I grew up in Chicago and came of age in the sixties. Chicago then was perhaps the most segregated northern city.

At age 15, I got my driver's license and my first real job. I went to work for a Jewish storeowner as a stock clerk for two years. Also during this era, high school sophomores in Chicago were required to read, "The Diary of Anne Frank," the autobiography written by a sixteen-year-old Jewish girl while she and her family hid from the Nazis in the attic of a home in Norway during World War II.

My Jewish boss, Al Cann, used to always say that I had good parents and when things were slow at the store, he would like to talk. We'd talk about life, careers, school, family, girls, sports, etc. On Saturdays, I would drive Al's new Oldsmobile Ninety-eight to South Shore, an affluent area of Chicago, to purchase corned beef and rye for lunch for the employees. Al would always comment about how much potential I had, everyone knew how much he liked me! He was like a second father to me, I certainly didn't have anything against Jews!

Also in those days, I would watch the World War II film footage depicting the horrors of the holocaust. So whenever Bruno would mention putting Jews in a microwave oven, I would picture the World War II death camps and crematory ovens.

It was kill or be killed, so I wrote a particularly bad report on the Jewish Youngstown wholesaler. Tom Johnson, the District Manager, had to follow up with his report. A market evaluation team was subsequently sent in to evaluate the wholesaler. A few weeks later, Michael Goldberg, the Jewish wholesaler, along with his attorney, were called to St. Louis, Missouri. Although I did not attend the meeting, I was told that Goldberg's attorney made absolute mincemeat of The Company attorneys. We were told after that, "Hands off" under any and all circumstances.

Boy, do I wish I could have attended that meeting. It's only November, and now the shit in Ohio was about to hit the fan. First, Richard Cline, the Region Manager, was demoted to Manager of Sales Training in St. Louis, Missouri. Almost the very same week, two managers walked into the Plant Manager's office at the Columbus brewing facility. They politely told him he was fired, watched while he packed his personal belongings, and on the spot accepted the keys to the plant and to his company car.

He had to call his wife to pick him up; that's how The Company operated. I was now developing a sense of fear about being fired. Richard Cline was replaced by Richard Stone, a middle aged man who seemed honest, earnest, and fair. I would soon learn that Richard should be in Hollywood and worthy of an Academy Award for his performance.

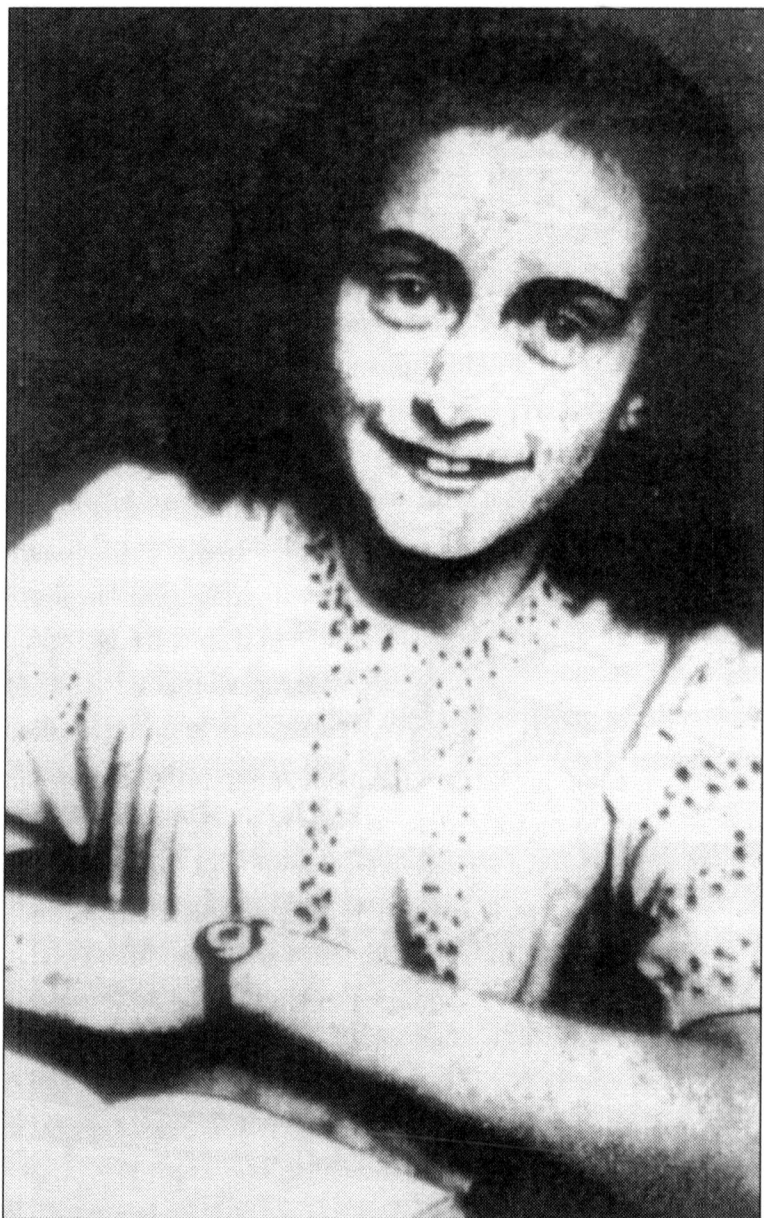

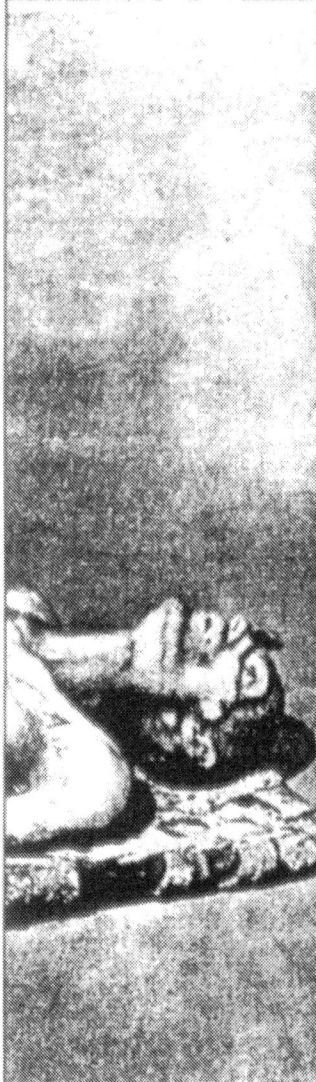

Thus the corpses of the murdered prisoners were burned.
Left: The corpse of a prisoner tortured to death in the camp.

C'est ainsi qu'on incinérait les corps des détenus assassinés au camp de concentration.
A gauche: le cadavre d'un détenu.

So wurden die Leichen der Häftlinge verbrannt.
Links: im Lager zu Tode gequält.

Pile of shoes from gassed Jewish victims, Lublin-Majdanek, 1945.

Crematorium ovens, Mauthausen KZ

The National Civil Rights Federation

The NCRF:

My Life As A Spy

4

I decided to contact the NCRF, The Columbus Chapter had just won a case to begin school busing in the city. I contacted Donald Falls, and after a brief conversation, he told me about Titus Marlowe's case against Bruno Pittman and The Company. It seems as though everyone was telling me about the Bruno Pittman situation. Mr. Falls suggested that I also contact Titus Marlowe, so I did. I called Titus that evening, and much to my surprise, he knew virtually everything about me. The Blacks from Chicago (his home-town) The Company, and the Central Distributing Company had been giving him all the details. It was decided that the safest place to meet was his attorney's house that Saturday afternoon. At the meeting were myself, Titus Marlowe and the attorney Scott Vaughn. I trusted them, but I sensed that they did not fully trust me. It was a casual afternoon, one would have thought we were assembled to watch a football game. We talked about the school busing case and basically, they just said to watch Bruno, that was it.

In the months following, there was a lot of traveling. I was very busy just trying to get accustomed to the paperwork and the drinking after hours. There was always an uneasiness, and the "deposition" of the District Managers and Personnel of Central Distributing Company became almost as commonplace as Bratbrau. I guess all or most of the sales and management employees of Central Distributing Company were depressed. The one Black salesman at the company, Chris Willis, was particularly affected. Because of the Titus Marlowe case, he felt his neck was on the chopping block. At the office, attorneys would disappear with the District Managers into the conference room to be deposed.

It's now around February 1979, and I had been employed by The Company for seven months, almost all I had done was work, so there was no time for anything else, and my bank account was starting to look pretty impressive. One day Bruno informed me that I had been selected for a special assignment at the region office, right outside of Chicago in Schaumberg, Illinois. Since I had a personal car as well as a company car, I was to fly every Monday to Chicago, drive the company car during the week, fly to Columbus on Fridays and drive my personal car on the weekends. My assignment was "administrator" for the conversion of the draft systems throughout the mid-west.

It was a breath of fresh air working in the region office; Richard Stone maintained an office as dignified as his manner. No depositions, no fears, no feeling compelled to go out and get drunk each evening. I was working with Ed Brown who is now a Brand Manager on the Bratbrau family of brands. We worked long hours, it was great; I loved every minute of it. I finally got a different look at The Company, and I could focus on improving The Company's stake in the industry. There were graphs; manpower projections; advertising; equipment; trips back and forth to St. Louis to coordinate and get approvals for the conversion from senior management. Finally, I didn't have to hurt anyone.

I would speak to Bruno periodically during this time. On one occasion, he asked me to come by the office when I got back to Columbus. That Friday evening, in his office, Bruno informed me that I had been approved to become a District Manager for a new district that was being developed, and that the assignment in Chicago was an opportunity (facade) for management to take a look at me firsthand. And that of course, I had exceeded their expectations. The new district would cover rural northwest Ohio, the wholesalers were located in Marion, Lorain, Bellevue, Delphos, Findlay, and I would have to move to Toledo, Ohio.

I was at the all too familiar crossroads, just like San Francisco, torn between exposure and reality. Now here I was in the limelight of The Company, being shuffled to isolation and ultimately to desolation. Just like l was told to move from Chicago to Columbus on his whim, now I was being told again to move without any consideration for my adaptability. That weekend in Columbus I once again considered resigning, the prospects of moving and living in Toledo, and the many days and nights I would have to spend in rural towns, was sickening.

By this time, it was also being rumored that part of the root causes for Titus Marlowe's demise was that his district was predominantly rural. To me, it was all too apparent. You did not have to be a social scientist to know that there were not only rural differences but cultural and social ones. It seemed so evident that I would be a "fish out of water" and totally out of my element in rural America. It was an area where I would find no McDonalds, convenience stores, department stores, or even theaters. If Bruno Pittman was so limited in his scope as to not realize the obvious problems I would have, then most assuredly senior management at The Company would know.

The Company was embroiled in a fight to the death with the Miller Brewing Company, a subsidiary of Phillip Morris Tobacco Company. Millers, with the aid of the mega-bucks Phillip Morris was pouring in, was beating The Company on all fronts. Miller Lite came virtually from nowhere to become the number two beer in the world. Miller High Life outsold Bratbrau in many markets in the country, including Ohio. Miller got a big jump on The Company by leaping into sports advertising. During the 1970's, the invigorated Milwaukee brewer gobbled up virtually every one of the major network sporting events, including the highly popular college football game of the week, the Moscow Olympics, the World Series, the Indianapolis 500, and dozens of college football games. Miller introduced segment marketing and advertising to the industry; they were the sole beer advertiser for Monday Night Football, which took the country by storm. Miller was also innovative in the packaging and introduction of 7 oz. bottles; 12-pack bottles; long neck N.R. bottles; and single valve draft cooperage. If all this wasn't enough, the company contracted with Lowenbrau of Germany, to brew the beer in the U.S.A., repositioned the price from Import to Super Premium, and to go head-to-head against The Company's floundering Leafbrau brand.

There was also a uniqueness about The Company, Inc. Family-owned and operated, the inside joke was that the "I-N-C" stood for "In-Laws, Nieces, and Cousins." The President and CEO, Hirsh H. Heidenthal, was himself a very unique individual. The industry tabloids stereotyped Hirsh as growing up isolated from society, then making a meteoric rise in the company, with what I would learn first hand was a result of his lifestyle and upbringing. His wealth isolated him from the realities of life for the average Black Manager. New employees learned that Hirsh did not like employees that smoked because Millers was a subsidiary of a tobacco company. During annual conventions and at meetings in St. Louis, Hirsh would focus on the Field Marketing Personnel. Hirsh would start grilling managers about their area of responsibility to which he would already have the answers, and typically, the poor bastards would be nervous and tongue-tied, and make mistakes and Hirsh would then smell blood and just go for the kill. You could look around the room and see stark fear on faces. Men would be sweating bullets. In fact, there was a joke that during one of these sessions, one manager seated towards the back of the room was observed praying.

Hirsh III's friend, and President of The Company, Inc., was Lantz L. Stone. It was during this time that the company "call" was implemented, "A Sense of Urgency." Employees were called upon to work longer and harder, to give their all, to ward off Miller Brewing Company. I myself was totally dedicated. I had not had an opportunity to go to movies, ball games, or dances with my peers. My only outlet had been the drinking sessions with Bruno Pittman and the office staff. The typical work week for Field Marketing Personnel was easily 70 to 90 hours. The Pennsylvania Business School concluded from its study that once again Field Marketing people were spending a lot of unproductive time typing the many reports that were due. Towards that end, each division office was authorized to have a typist do the Area and District Managers' typing.

Helen Barken was hired while I was on assignment in Chicago, we were introduced via the phone but it was some time before I would be in the Columbus office during normal business hours to actually meet her. Around April 1, 1979, virtually all of the Black Area Managers were summoned to the Region III office. There were of course, Mel Hunter from Chicago, Rick Gates from Detroit, Pat Hodges from Washington, D.C., John Knight from St. Louis, and Phillip White from New Orleans. The Blacks were called in to interview with Bruno Pittman and Richard Stone for the Toledo position.

I guess it was no wonder why The Company had no credibility with Black employees. That evening when we were able to get together with just ourselves, we talked of the charade of interviewing for first, a position that had already been filled by me, and second, what Black person in their right mind would want to work for Bruno "Little Hitler" Pittman and live in Toledo, Ohio. It was openly discussed that The Company only wanted a Black so that it would look good for Bruno Pittman at the impending trial. The guys even told of the elaborate stories they invented to explain why they should not be considered for the position. Pat Hodges said that his son was nearing his senior year in high school, and to relocate would diminish his chances of a football scholarship. There were all kinds of excuses, from wives' employment, to wanting to stay close to a sick mother. It was as if we were the Christians pulling straws, and the one with the shortest straw (me) had to face the lions in the Coliseum. I can remember the evening ending with a lot of "good lucks" and pats on the back—too bad they could not hide the pity in their eyes. The next day, Richard Stone and Bruno Pittman told me that I had been selected as the official "sacrifice." I asked about the training and once again got the shock of my life when Richard Stone, this trustworthy guy, looked me straight in the eye and said, "A guy of your talent doesn't need any training." To give you some scope of the District Manager's position, Whites are designated Division Representatives, and the training is six months. For Blacks, it's either sink or swim.

We decided to use Columbus, Ohio as our first test market for the draft conversion in May. The bugs for the conversion would be worked out in Columbus, before converting throughout the country. Approximately 40 of The Company's field marketing managers descended on Columbus. While the conversion took about a week and was a great success, something significant took place that week. That was my introduction to Helen Barken. We had talked several times during her employment, but this was my first opportunity to see and meet her. Helen was a middle-aged, blue-eyed blonde who was divorced and had two pre-teen daughters. She epitomized middle class in middle America. Helen looked the part of an The Company employee; her only ostensible flaw, if any, was that she was divorced. Helen was warm and friendly. She had a sincere interest in The Company. She was a genuine person.

While working in Chicago, the new draft system was dubbed Tri-Tap. "3" stood for single, safe and sanitary. During the conversion week, the Division staff went out at least a couple of times. Lynn would call a girlfriend from The Company Brewing Plant a couple of blocks away. The three girls, Helen, Lynn and her friend, were then nicknamed: Single, Safe and Sanitary. We went out to celebrate the success of the conversion, Helen's employment, and my promotion. We hit several bars on the north end of Columbus. We would drink, dance, our drinking did not cease until it was time for the bars to close.

District XXX was to become effective June 1, 1979. In only two weeks I would become only the fourth or fifth Black District Manager ever in the company, by far and away the youngest Black at age 28. Bruno commented that as far as he was concerned, I no longer had to worry about the Black markets in Ohio. In hindsight, I had two weeks before the beginning of the end, but I was about to make another grave mistake.

Alliance

5

With only a few weeks to get training, I was getting desperate. I asked Robert Gladstone if I could come to Cincinnati to train with him. Robert was a middle-aged man who had been a District Manager for another brewery. He was from St. Louis, had attended private high school with the President of The Company, and had been an officer in the U.S. Marines. His wife, Jane, was independently wealthy and they lived in a mansion on the Ohio river. While Robert never questioned or disputed Bruno in my presence, everyone knew that Robert's wealth and background intimidated Bruno. On my weekly itinerary, I listed that I would be in Cincinnati the following week. Bruno confronted me with why was I going to Cincinnati? When I informed him I was going to train with Robert, he replied that Robert was too busy to be working with me. My world was coming apart. I was by now so disillusioned.

I didn't want to believe that I was being destined for failure. If The Company was in a battle almost for survival,

why would they jeopardize this by not training me? I decided
to call Donald Falls at the NCRF. He agreed to meet me, this
time with a colleague, Pat Lawrence. It was evident that Bruno
was trying to manipulate me in anticipation of the Titus
Marlowe trial. The two men were sure that I would be called
on to testify on Bruno's behalf. After all, with all the mistakes I
was sure to make by not being trained, Bruno could be
benevolent, and I would be in his debt. In a subsequent
meeting with Titus Marlowe and his attorney Mr. Vaughn, I
was shown some of the letters and memos pertaining to Titus
Marlowe's discrimination case against Bruno Pittman and The
Company. At this meeting, I was shown Titus Marlowe's
evaluations prior to Bruno Pittman becoming his boss. For
fourteen and a half years he had received only the highest of
evaluations. I read a letter (Exhibit A) written by Sonia M.
Norville, Lynn Thaxton's predecessor. Ms. Norville had been
secretary to the Division Manager prior to Bruno—Mr. John R.
Pascal. Excerpts from the letter are attached."

"Over a period of five years, I found Titus to be a very
conscientious, hard working employee. He was very anxious to
please and was very cooperative with everyone. His work was
always in on time and also accurate. On occasions I would
remind the District Managers of reports due and again, in these
instances, Titus was very cooperative and responsive, sometimes even more so than the other District Managers.

"When Titus's appointment to District Manager in this
area was announced, one of our wholesalers, Mr. Harvey
Mednick, was very upset and called on Mr. Pascal to voice his
concerns. Mr. Mednick stated that this area was not ready for a
Black District Manager and he definitely did not want one in

his District. Mr. Pascal repeated this to me after Mr. Mednick left the office, stating Mr. Mednick was still very upset.

"Also during that period of time, Mr. Mednick wrote a letter complaining about the lack of point of sale items in his District and used the word "niggardly" in the letter. Mr. Pascal was very angry and chastised Mr. Mednick for the usage, stating under the circumstances, it was considered insulting."

In 1977, Titus Marlowe wrote a market report, as required, on Mednick Distributing Company. In Mr. Mednick's reply to Bruno Pittman's follow-up letter, he stated he would correct the problems pointed out in the report. Mr. Mednick also added: "About March 15, 1977, I realized that Titus Marlowe had not called on us this year. I mentioned this to Mark Geiger, our Cambridge Manager, and asked him to keep a record of Marlowe's visits to Cambridge. Here is the record:

March 22-1 hour (7-8 a.m.) Showed the 1977 advertising film. Left for ___ Ohio.

April 12-2 hours (9-11 a.m.) Left alone at 11 a.m. to check the market.

April 13-3 hours (9-12 noon) Left to go to _____.

April 14-2 hours (11-1 p.m.) Left alone at 1 p.m. for lunch and to check the market.

"Cambridge is the second largest market in Mr. Marlowe's district. On this seventh day of June, he has spent 8 hours in our office and warehouse this year of 1977. He has not made a call with our salesman, nor has he been on a route truck with our driver-salesman this year. You might have had Mr. Marlowe assigned to other markets during the past five months. If this is the reason we have not seen him, we hope the situation will change. We will welcome the opportunity to work more with our District Manager and have his knowledge, criticism, and assistance in solving any problem we might have in our operations."

Was it worth all of this for Titus Marlowe to stick it out? The man was in a red neck District, where he was uncomfortable both in the wholesalers operation as well as the marketplace. It would come to my mind in future years in a similar type of environment if I indeed would be setup by the wholesaler, by The Company, or both!

As a result of Harvey Mednick's letter, Titus had to refute the allegations made by a man who did not want a Black District Manager, and who used the word niggardly in conversations and documentation. Exhibit E shows that between January and June 1st, Titus Marlowe had spent eight weeks out of the state on special assignment, and that based on the equation that determines the amount of time a District Manager is to spend in each market, Titus had exceeded the number of days warranted in Mednick's market.

Dear Mr. ████

I worked with ████████ at ████████████ for approximately
five (5) years. I was the secretary to the Division Sales Manager,
Mr. ████████ and ███ was one of three District Managers who
reported to the Division Manager. All of the District Managers' work
came through me. I noted whether it was in on time, whether it was
correct, etc., then handled it accordingly.

During that period of time I found ███ to be a very conscientious,
hard working employee. He was very anxious to please and very cooperative with everyone. His work was always in on time and also
accurate. On occassion I would remind the District Managers of
reports due and again, in these instances, ███ was very cooperative
and responsive, sometimes even more so than the other District Managers.

When ████ appointment to District Manager in this area was announced,
one of our Wholesalers, Mr. ████████, was very upset and called
on Mr. ████ personally to voice his concern. Mr. ████████ stated
that this area was not ready for a black District Manager and he
definitely did not want one in his District. Mr. ████ repeated this
to me after Mr. ████████ left the office, stating Mr. ████████ was
still very upset.

Also during that period of time, Mr. ████████ wrote a letter complaining
about the lack of Point of Sale items in his District and used the word,
"niggardly" in the letter. Mr. ████ was very angry and chastised Mr.
████████ for the usage, stating under the circumstances, it was considered insulting.

Generally speaking, it was my impression that ████████ was well
liked and respected by all the Wholesalers he called upon. We had no
complaints against him while I was there.

Sincerely yours,

Dear ▮▮▮

In reply to your letter of June 1, 1977 concerning five items on a
market report of our ▮▮▮▮ operation by the District Manager,
Mr. ▮▮▮▮, we offer the following:

1. Our Draught Prospect list for each route was with our salesmen.
In the future, the actual Draught Prospect cards will be in the
office and the information for each account will be in the salesman's
route book. The information was over 90% correct and the other
10% is being up-dated.

2. One of our salesman's volume summary was incomplete. We had a
review of the salesmen route books with our salesmen, and we know
this problem is being corrected.

3. Our personnel have recently attended marketing and management
seminars, sponsored by the Wholesale Beer Association of Ohio.
We will continue to avail ourselves of opportunities to further
our knowledge and expertise in the operation of our business.

4. We had no firm plans for an environmentally controlled warehouse at the time Mr. ▮▮▮▮ asked me. We now are proceeding to
insulate our entire warehouse to a thermal factor, that will be
more than adequate for environmental control.

5. One out of five driver- salesmen has been negligent in filling
out his route book. This situation is now being corrected.

Page 2

About March 15, 1977, I realized that ████████ had not called on us this year. I mentioned this to████████, our ███████.Manager, and asked him to keep a record of █████ visits to ██████.

Here is the record:

March 22 - 1 hour (7-8am) Showed the 1977 Advertising Film. Left for ███████, Ohio.
April 12 - (2)hours (9-11 am) Left alone at 11:00 am to check the market.
April 13 - 3 hours (9-12 noon) Left to go to ████████.
April 14 - 2 hours (11-1 pm) Left alone at 1:00 pm for lunch and to check the market.

████████ is the second largest market in Mr. ████████ district. On this seventh day of June, he has spent 8 hours in our office and warehouse this year of 1977. He has not made a call with our salesmen nor has he been on a route truck with our driver-salesmen this year.

You might have had Mr. ███████ assigned to other markets during the past five months. If this is the reason we have not seen him, we hope the situation will change. We will welcome the opportunity to work more with our District Manager, and have his knowledge, criticism, and assistance in solving any problems we might have in our operations.

Sincerely yours,

cc ████████
   ████████

EXHIBIT B

To refute Mr. ███████████ reference to the number of days
I spent in his market, the following is reflective of the special
assignment that I was engaged in for the first six months of 1977.

PLACE	ACTIVITY	DATE
Lansing, Michigan	Intro.███████████	2-5-77
Detroit, Michigan	Operation Blitz	5-17-77
Cleveland, Ohio	Operation Blitz	5-7-77
Chicago, Illinois	Operation Blitz	2-21-77
St. Louis, Missouri	Seminar	5-24-77
New Orleans, Louisiana	Seminar	3-17-77
Williamsburg, Virginia	Operation Blitz	6-2-77
District ██████	Intro. 1977 Media	3-21-77

Out of a total of 110 working days, 43 days were spent
on special assignment in 1977. This equates to 39% of total number
of working days prior to my termination. ████████, Ohio represented
8.9% of District ████ volume. Based on volume versus time, this
constituted spending approximately six working days within the
████████, Ohio market area. I spent seven working days within the
████████, Ohio marketing area.

███████████████

█████████████

ON TUESDAY, ███████████████, DIVISION REPRESENTATIVE ██████████████ AND I CALLED ON OUR WHOLESALER IN ████████, OHIO, FOR THE PURPOSE OF ON-GOING TRAINING AND TO DISCUSS WITH OUR WHOLESALER CERTAIN MARKETING PROBLEMS.

AT MY REQUEST, ██████ COMPLETED AN "ANALYSIS OF SPECIFIC MARKET REVIEW" AS PART OF HIS TRAINING ACTIVITIES.

████████████████ COMPLETED A MARKET REPORT ON FEBRUARY 19, 1977, AND AN "ANALYSIS OF SPECIFIC MARKET REVIEW" ON FEBRUARY 28, 1977.

A REVIEW OF █████████ REPORT REVEALS A DIFFERENT EVALUATION OF THE WHOLESALER'S OPERATION THAN THAT OF █████████ REPORT.

FOR THE RECORD, I REVIEWED THE RESULTS OF THE REPORT WITH ████████ IN THE WHOLESALER'S OFFICE TO MAKE SURE ██████████ OBSERVATIONS WERE CORRECT. SEE ATTACHED COPIES OF █████████ REPORT AND ████████████ REPORT.

WE FEEL THIS VERIFIES OUR SUSPICIONS THAT ███████ DOES NOT REPORT PROBLEMS IN THE WHOLESALER'S OPERATIONS FOR POSSIBLY TWO REASONS:

1. ████████ DOES NOT REVIEW IN DETAIL ALL FACETS OF THE OPERATION WHILE MAKING MARKET CALLS, OR

2. ████████ DOES NOT CARE TO STATE FACTS AS REQUIRED BY ████ POLICIES.

████████████████████

████████   ████████████

████████████████████

MR. ██████████████████

PLEASE PLAN TO BE IN THE DIVISION OFFICE ON
THURSDAY, MAY 19, 1977, AT 9:30 A.M. TO MEET
WITH ████████████ AND MYSELF.

████████████████

██████████

CC: ████████████████

THIS WILL CONFIRM OUR MEETING ON THE ABOVE DATE
IN THIS OFFICE WITH ▮▮▮▮▮▮▮▮ AND MYSELF.

WE DISCUSSED YOUR UNSATISFACTORY WORK PERFORMANCE
AND THE REASONS FOR THE PROBATION PERIOD. AT THE
CONCLUSION OF THE MEETING YOU ACKNOWLEDGED THAT
YOU UNDERSTOOD ALL OF THE REASONS AND THE TERMS
OF THE PROBATION.

IF YOU HAVE ANY QUESTIONS RELATED TO YOUR PERFOR-
MANCE DURING THE PROBATION PERIOD, FEEL FREE TO
CONTACT THIS OFFICE OR THE REGION OFFICE.

▇▇▇▇▇▇▇▇

Mr. ▇▇▇▇▇▇▇▇

YOUR PERFORMANCE SINCE MAY, 1976, THROUGH MAY 10, 1977, IN THE OPINION OF THIS OFFICE, HAS BEEN LESS THAN SATISFACTORY. SOME OF THE REASONS FOR THIS UNSATISFACTORY PERFORMANCE WERE DISCUSSED WITH YOU ON THE ABOVE DATE IN THIS OFFICE.

AS A RESULT OF THIS UNSATISFACTORY PERFORMANCE, YOU ARE HEREBY NOTIFIED THAT YOU ARE BEING PLACED ON PROBATION IN ACCORDANCE WITH THE PERSONNEL POLICIES OF ▇▇▇▇▇▇▇▇ THIS PERIOD OF PROBATION WILL EXTEND FROM THIS DATE TO AUGUST 10, 1977. DURING THIS PERIOD YOUR WORK WILL BE EVAL- UATED ON A CONTINUOUS BASIS. YOU MAY INQUIRE RE- GARDING YOUR PERFORMANCE AT ANY TIME DURING THIS PERIOD.

IF, BY AUGUST 10, 1977, YOU HAVE NOT SHOWN A MARKED IMPROVEMENT, IN THE OPINION OF MANAGEMENT, YOUR EMPLOYMENT WITH ▇▇▇▇▇▇▇▇, WILL BE TERMINATED.

IF YOU SHOW IMPROVEMENT, AS WE HOPE YOU WILL, YOU WILL BE ALLOWED TO CONTINUE YOUR EMPLOYMENT WITH ▇▇▇▇▇▇▇▇, WITH ALL TERMS AND CONDITIONS AFFORDED OTHER EMPLOYEES WHO ARE RATED SATISFACTORY.

ADDITIONALLY, YOU ARE EXPECTED TO COMMUNICATE TO THIS OFFICE ANY AND ALL CHANGES IN ROUTING VIA THE FIELD MAN'S ROUTE LIST AND/OR BY TELEPHONE. THE MIDWESTERN REGION POLICY NUMBER 3 CLEARLY EXPLAINS THE ARRIVAL AND DEPARTURE TIMES YOU ARE TO BE IN A MARKET. AS YOU KNOW, THIS OFFICE, THE REGION AND ▇▇▇▇ OFFICES HAVE HOURS OF 8:30 A.M. TO 5:00 P.M. WE EXPECT YOUR MARKET ACTIVITIES TO COINCIDE WITH THESE HOURS. ANY ADMINISTRATIVE TIME SPENT AT HOME ON ADMINISTRATIVE DUTIES ARE TO BE LISTED ON THE DAILY TRADE CALL REPORT AND IN ACCORDANCE WITH MIDWESTERN REGION POLICY NUMBER 1.

EXHIBIT D

Please note ▆▆▆▆▆▆▆ letter of May 10, 1977, stating that, "Your performance since May, 1976, through May 10, 1977, in the opinion of this office, has been less than satisfactory. Some of the reasons for this unsatisfactory performance were discussed with you on the above date in this office." The contents of this letter was never discussed with me by▆▆▆▆▆▆ at any time in my employment with ▆▆▆▆▆▆▆▆▆▆▆

Also, please refer to my Employee Appraisal of October 8, 1976, in which an evaluation of GOOD to VERY GOOD was arrived at by ▆▆▆▆▆. This definitely points to ▆▆▆▆▆▆ dishonest character as well exposing his continued falsehoods relative to my performance and ability.

Other factors that also prove my claim of discriminatory treatment in ▆▆▆▆▆▆ appraisal are as follows:

1. During a period beginning in February and continuing through the month of June, I worked in the ▆▆▆▆▆ brewery during the ▆▆▆▆▆ strike of 1976. (12 hrs. a day/ 7 days per wk.)

2. For a period of two weeks upon the conclusion of the strike, I was employed in the Inventory Programming Department as a coordinator. I was the only District Manager that was assigned to this duty for that length of time.

3. For a period of one week in September of 1976, 1

⟨TO BE REVISED⟩ oy ▮▮▮▮▮▮▮

▮▮▮ CONFIDENTIAL EMPLOYEE APPRAISAL   Tentative preparation date ▮▮▮▮▮▮▮

Final preparation date ....

▮▮▮▮▮▮▮ ....   PREPARED BY ▮▮▮▮▮▮▮

Group No. P-2   Dept. MARKETING ....Date employed ..11/1/62/

Present Position DISTRICT MANAGER   Salary Grade 19   Time in this Position ..44 MONTHS.   Consulting with ....

1. Evaluate employee's performance in PRESENT POSITION. Place check mark or an "X" in most applicable block.

	UNSATISFACTORY	SATISFACTORY BUT NEEDS IMPROVEMENT	GOOD	VERY GOOD	EXCELLENT	NOT A...
KNOWLEDGE OF WORK:				X		
QUALITY OF WORK:			X			
VOLUME OF WORK:			X			
COMMUNICATION:		X				
FOLLOW THROUGH:				X		
PLANNING & ORGANIZATION:				X		
JUDGEMENT:			X			
ANALYTICAL ABILITY:			X			
CREATIVITY:			X			
DEPENDABILITY:				X		
INITIATIVE:			X			
COOPERATION & RELATIONSHIPS:			X			
ATTITUDE & FLEXIBILITY:		X				
PERSONALITY:				X		
DEVELOPMENT OF SUBORDINATES:						
LEADERSHIP:			X			
Supervisor's discretion, explain in remarks						

CONFIDENTIAL EMPLOYEE APPRAISAL

Date _____

	Name _____	Present Position ___ DISTRICT MANAGER	Time in this Position ___ MAR.

Group ___ P-2 ___ Date of Employment ___ NOVEMBER 1, 1962 ___ PREPARED BY: _____ Consulting with _____

Consider employee's performance in *PRESENT POSITION*. Description of items to be rated is on reverse. Place check mark in middle of most applicable block or on appropriate line between blocks if appraisal on any item is intermediate. If necessary, amplify in the REMARKS section on reverse.

Indicate if the REMARKS section was used

YES ☐
NO ☒

EXCELLENT											N/A	N/A			
GOOD	X	X	X	X	X	X			X		X		X	X	X
SATISFACTORY															
NEEDS IMPROVEMENT															
UNSATISFACTORY															

13. CONCERNING EMPLOYEE'S PRESENT ASSIGNMENT: — SUPERVISOR: (Indicate) PRESENTLY _____ POTENTIAL X ___ NOT APPLICABLE ___

A. Do you feel this employee is properly placed? ___ YES ___ If not, explain briefly: _____

B. Indicate the employee's overall job performance: Excellent ___ Good X ___ Satisfactory ___ Needs Improvement ___ Unsatisfactory ___

14. CONCERNING EMPLOYEE'S FUTURE:

A. Does employee have potential for further advancement? (If YES, complete rest of page. If NO, explain in REMARKS section.) YES

B. What are employee's outstanding abilities (assignments on which employee has excelled, etc.)? EMPLOYEE IS COMPETENT, CAPABLE AND AMBITIOUS.

C. What are employee's weak points (personal characteristics or assignments on which employee has not proved satisfactory, etc.)? NONE

D. For what type assignment does employee appear a candidate for advancement in present or other department or subsidiary: (1) Next assignment? _____ (2) Eventual? REGION ADMINISTRATOR

E. What training or experience is necessary to qualify employee for such next assignment? ADDITIONAL EXPOSURE AND TRAINING

F. Is any such training contemplated and if so, when? CURRENTLY RECEIVING TRAINING AND EXPOSURE

G. When will employee be ready for next assignment indicated? TWO YEARS

In fact, I was shown many documents that clearly ill-
ustrated that Bruno was determined to fire Titus Marlowe
at any price. Exhibit F and F1 is an Ohio Civil Rights
Commission Discharge Questionnaire and Titus Marlowe's
refutation of Bruno Pittman's response to the questionnaire.

Exhibit F1—"Please note Mr. Pittman's response to
questions 23 on the last page of the Ohio Civil Rights
Commission Discharge Questionnaire. The question states that
during the last two years, how many employees have been
given warnings or less than discharge for the type of conduct
which gives rise to the discharge for complaint? Mr. Pittman's
response to the question was "none." This response is difficult
to comprehend when we are both aware that Leo Sampson was
in fact placed on probation in March/April of 1976. The date of
the questionnaire is November of 1977, a full year after Mr.
Sampson was placed on probation."

From the many memos it was clear that Titus Marlowe
had proof that Bruno Pittman had falsified records and memos
with the sole intent of terminating Marlowe's employment with
The Company.

20. If one reason for Complainant's discharge was absenteeism or tardiness, attach a copy of Complainant's attendance and sick day record. NO, NOT ABSENTEEISM OR TARDINESS AS WE RELATE IT TO BEING LATE FOR WORK OR NOT SHOWING UP AT ALL. HOWEVER, ABSENTEEISM, AS WE WOULD DESCRIBE IT, WHICH HAS BEEN DOCUMENTED (SEE FILE) AND VARIFIED BY AT LEAST TWO OF OUR WHOLE-SALERS COULD BEST DESCRIBE LEAVING WHOLESALER ON NUMEROUS OCCASIONS AND RETURNING HOME WHICH GENERALLY CONSTITUTED ONE HALF DAY IN WORK HOURS & PRODUCTIVI

21. Did Complainant ever complain of receiving discriminatory treatment on the job? NOT AS IT WOULD BE RELATED TO HIS ACTIVITIES WITHIN THE CONFINES OF THE DIVISION OFFICE OR AT ANY TIME OR IN ANY MANNER DURING MY MARKET CALL ACTIVITIES WITH EMPLOYEE. HOWEVER, EMPLOYEE DID COMPLAIN ON AT LEAST TWO OCCASIONS OF RECEIVING DISCRIMINATORY TREATMENT AT THE HANDS OF CERTAIN RETAIL ACCOUNTS IN SOUTHERN OHIO.

22. If the answer to the above is yes, specify the nature of the complaint, date(s) of complaint, and explain what was done pursuant to the complaint. EMPLOYEE COMPLAINED THAT CERTAIN RETAILERS HAD MADE CERTAIN DISCRIMINATORY REMARKS REGARDING RACE WHILE EMPLOYEE WAS MAKING RETAIL CALLS IN THE ▮▮▮▮▮▮▮▮▮▮▮▮▮▮▮▮▮ MARKETS. NOTHING COULD BE DONE BY MY OFFICE TO EFFECT A CHANGE OF ATTITUDE ON BEHALF OF RETAIL OUTLETS.

23. (a) During the last two (2) years, how many employees have been given warnings or penalties of less than discharge for the type of conduct which gave rise to the discharge of Complainant? Indicate for each the name, address, phone number, jurisdictional description*, date of hire, date of warning(s) or penalty, and the circumstances.

    NONE

    (b) During the last two (2) years, how many employees have been discharged for the type of conduct which gave rise to the discharge of Complainant? Indicate for each the name, address, phone number, and jurisdictional description*.

    NONE

*See last paragraph of page one.

EXHIBITS I CONT.

Please note ▓▓▓▓▓▓▓▓▓▓▓▓ to question 23 on the
last page of the <u>OHIO CIVIL RIGHTS COMMISSION DISCHARGE QUESTIONNAIRE</u>.
The question states that "During the last two years, how many
employees have been given warnings or penalties of less than discharge
for the type of conduct which gave rise to the discharge of complainant?"
▓▓▓▓▓▓▓▓▓▓ response to the question was "none." This response is
difficult to comprehend when we are both aware that ▓▓▓▓▓▓▓▓
was in fact placed on probation in March/April of 1976. The date
of the questionnaire is November of 1977, a full year after ▓▓▓▓▓▓▓
was placed on probation.

A June 29, 1977 memo to file written by Bruno Pittman and received by The Company "Equal Opportunity/Affairs" office on July 11, 1977 contained more allegations:

Exhibit G1—"On Tuesday, June 28, 1977, while continuing a Market Swing in District XXX, comments were made by Mr. Albert Hartman, General Manager of Fairfax Distributing Company, in the presence of Mr. Ronald Kirsh, President of Fairfax, our Lexington, Ohio Wholesaler, as follows:

A discussion regarding The Company and wholesaler pricing. At that time Mr. Hartman said that Marlowe told him that he (Marlowe) would tell him when to raise prices and how much. I am not sure that those were the exact words used due to the length of time it took Mr. Hartman to complete his story. However, the general tone of Mr. Hartman's comments indicated that Marlowe did in fact make a statement to that effect.

"Marlowe spent very little time in the market with Salesmen and/or Driver/Salesmen" or they described the time he spent as "late arrival and early departure."

The above comments were voluntarily spoken to me by Messrs. Howard Ferguson, Bayton; Jim Ingram, Dexter City; and Albert Hartman, Watertown. Our wholesalers in Quaker City, Somerton, and Winchester did not volunteer any comments."

Exhibit H1 is Titus Marlowe's response to the memo to file-second paragraph:

"My attorney and myself confronted both of the above mentioned wholesalers in reference to this quote. They both emphatically denied making this statement to Mr. Pittman. My attorney and I have a taped statement from each wholesaler that totally refutes Mr. Pittman's statement. This again illustrates the fabrication of lies by Mr. Pittman. The above may be confirmed by telephoning Mr. Ferguson at (XXX) XXX-XXXX and/or Mr. Ingram at (XXX) XXX-XXXX regarding this statement."

Bruno Pittman in a memo to filed regarding Exhibit I:

"Incidents where Marlowe disregards Division's Instructions." 2). "We requested all District Managers to submit menus for Post Convention for consideration. Marlowe disregarded this request and booked a sit-down dinner. Our reasoning was that a buffet dinner could be served inexpensively and in a better fashion than a sit-down dinner. When asked why he didn't follow through, he explained that, in his opinion, the buffet dinner was no cheaper than a sit-down dinner and became indignant about our questioning his judgment regarding the situation.

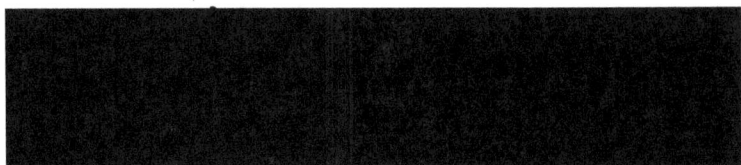

ON TUESDAY, JUNE 28, 1977, WHILE CONTINUING A
MARKET SWING IN DISTRICT ████, COMMENTS WERE MADE
BY ████████████████, GENERAL MANAGER OF ████████
███████████████ IN THE PRESENCE OF ████████████
██████, PRESIDENT OF █████████████████████████████
OHIO WHOLESALER, AS FOLLOWS:

█████████████ RELATED THAT IN JANUARY, SHORTLY AFTER
THE DECISION OF ████████████████ MANAGEMENT TO INCREASE
F.O.B.'S BY 1% WAS UNDERSTOOD BY ████ WHOLESALERS,
█████████████ CALLED ON OUR ████████████ WHOLESALER
AND AT SOME POINT DURING THE VISIT ENTERED INTO
A DISCUSSION REGARDING ████ AND WHOLESALER PRICING.
AT THAT TIME ████████ SAID THAT ████████ TOLD HIM
THAT HE ████████ WOULD TELL HIM WHEN TO RAISE
PRICES AND HOW MUCH. I AM NOT SURE THAT THOSE
WERE THE EXACT WORDS USED DUE TO THE LENGTH OF
TIME IT TOOK ████████████ TO COMPLETE HIS STORY,
HOWEVER, THE GENERAL TONE OF █████████████ COMMENTS
INDICATED THAT ████████ DID IN FACT MAKE A STATEMENT
TO THAT EFFECT. █████████████ HAD AT LEAST TWO WIT-
NESSES TO THE CONVERSATION AND WE ARE REASONABLY
SURE THAT HE WOULD BE WILLING TO EXPLAIN THE DIS-
CUSSION IN DETAIL WITH ANYONE WHO WOULD REQUEST
ADDITIONAL INFORMATION.

DURING THE WEEK OF JUNE 27, 1977, █████████████, REGION
MANAGER, WAS ON VACATION. IN HIS ABSENCE, I CALLED
MR. ████████████████████ AND RELATED █████████████
COMMENTS TO HIM REGARDING THE █████████████ PRICE
CONVERSATION. MR. █████████ ADVISED ME TO MAKE SURE
THAT OUR WHOLESALER UNDERSTOOD THAT ████████ APPROACH
TO THE PRICING DISCUSSION WAS NOT IN LINE WITH ████
POLICY AND TO ASSURE OUR █████████████ WHOLESALER
THAT WE, █████████████, DID NOT THEN NOR WILL WE
IN THE FUTURE SANCTION SUCH ACTIONS. I STATED THAT
THIS HAD ALREADY BEEN EXPLAINED TO OUR WHOLESALER
BY ME PRIOR TO MY LEAVING THE MARKET. #1

PAGE 2

████████████

COMMENTS FROM WHOLESALERS IN DISTRICT ███ REGARDING ████████ WERE NOT SOLICITED BY ME AT ANY TIME. COMMENTS THAT WERE MADE BY OUR WHOLESALER PRINCIPLES AND/OR SALES MANAGERS WERE IN GENERAL:

████████ SPENT VERY LITTLE TIME IN THE MARKET WITH SALESMEN AND/OR DRIVER/SALESMEN" OR THEY DESCRIBED THE TIME HE SPENT IN THE MARKET AS "LATE ARRIVAL (AFTER 9:00), EARLY DEPARTURE (USUALLY AROUND 12 TO 1:00), AND WHEN HE DID LEAVE THE OPERATION TO WORK IN THE MARKET, IT WAS GENERALLY ALONE".

THE ABOVE COMMENTS WERE VOLUNTARILY SPOKEN TO ME BY MESSRS: ████████████████████████████████ ████████████████ AND ████████████████████ ████████ OUR WHOLESALERS IN ████████████████ ████████ DID NOT VOLUNTER ANY COMMENTS.

████████████████████████████

████████████████

████████

CC: ████████████████████████

EXHIBITS E

Please note Mr.████████ memo to file dated June 29, 1977.
On page 2, ████████ states that ████████, ████████████,
and ████████████████████, made the statement that ████████
spent very little time in the market with salesmen and/or driver.'
salesmen or they described the time he spent in the market as late
arrival (after 9:00), early departure (usually around 12 to 1:00)."

My attorney and myself confronted both of the above
mentioned wholesalers in reference to this quote. They both
emphatically denied making this statement to Mr.████████ My attorney
and I have a taped statement from each wholesaler that totally
refutes Mr████████ statement. This again illustrates the
fabrication of lies by Mr.████████. The above may be confirmed by
telephoning Mr████████ at ████████████ and/or Mr.████████ at
████████████ regarding this statement.

Once again in Titus Marlowe's response Exhibit 1:

Item 2). "The Post Convention was a buffet dinner and not a sit-down dinner as stated by Mr. Pittman. I have the billing from the Hilton Inn North to confirm that the dinner was in fact a buffet dinner."

Titus Marlowe was answering one accusation or another, the memos to file; St. Louis Headquarters; the Equal Opportunity Affair department—too numerous to go into detail. But briefly Titus was admonished for using the copy machine at the plant (Exhibit J), expense reports (Exhibit K), his itinerary (Exhibit I). Titus Marlowe was even admonished for sending a form to the wrong department. All of this while he was working twelve hour shifts, 7 days a week in the plant during the strike.

I can't imagine how Titus Marlowe kept the hectic pace, the traveling by car and airplane, the administration, the mental strain of working in a rural marketplace. How soon I would learn what it was like to be Black and go into a bar in the land of pickup trucks and rebel flags! The precarious feeling of walking into a hostile business that employed no Blacks, or minorities, where the sentiment of overt racism was displayed by the owner, permeated the entire operation.

Mr. ██████████

DURING OUR RETURN TRIP FROM THE ███████████ MARKET ON NOVEMBER ███ 1976, WE ENGAGED IN A CASUAL CONVERSATION REGARDING YOUR CONSIDERATION FOR YOUR POSSIBLE PURCHASE OF A NEW AUTOMOBILE. IN YOUR WORDS YOU STATED THAT YOU HAD 45,000 MILES ON YOUR CURRENT AUTO. A GLANCE AT THE ODOMETER PROVED YOU RIGHT WITH MILEAGE AT THAT TIME OF 44,980.

A REVIEW OF YOUR EXPENSE REPORT DATED WEEK ENDING 12/4/76 SHOWS YOUR ENDING MILEAGE TO BE 31,991.

A FURTHER CHECK OF YOUR EXPENSE REPORTS FROM THE WEEK ENDING 4/12/75 TO DATE REVEALS THE FOLLOWING. SEE ATTACHMENT.

ON OR BEFORE JANUARY 3, 1977, PLEASE SEND THIS OFFICE AN EXPLANATION FOR MILEAGE DISCREPANCIES AND YOUR REASONS FOR NOT REPORTING YOUR MILEAGE CORRECTLY FROM 4/12/75 TO DATE.

1975	Date	Mileage	Date	Mileage	Date	Mileage
	4/ 5	69,452	7/ 5	6,051	10/11	11,485
	4/12	841	7/12	6,672	10/18	12,276
	4/19	1,497	7/19	7,328	10 25	12,676
	4/26	2,180	8/ 2	7,923	11/ 1	13,417
	5/ 3	2,967	8/ 9	7,963	11/ 8	14,137
	5/10	3,495	8/16	2,993	11/15	13,540
	5/17	3,688	8/23	6,684	11/22	14,240
	5/24	3,708	8/30	7,376	11/29	VACATION
	5/31	4,197	9/ 6	7,976	12/ 6	15,290
	6/ 7	4,217	9/13	8,676	12/13	16,032
	6/14	4,872	9/20	9,536	12/20	16,532
	6/21	4,884	9/27	10,125	12/27	16,732
	6/28	5,491	10/ 4	10,816		

1975 TOTAL MILES PER REPORTS: (19,780)

1976	Date	Mileage	Date	Mileage	Date	Mileage
	1/ 3	16,782	4/24	20,223	8/28	VACATION
	1/10	17,342	5/ 1	20,293	9/ 4	VACATION
	1/17	17,780	5/ 8	11,315	9/11	17,041
	1/24	18,240	5/22	11,490	9/18	17,671
	1/31	18,690	6/ 5	11,605	9/25	17,871
	2/ 7	18,730	6/12	12,781	10/ 9	24,720
	2/14	19,180	6/19	13,331	10/16	25,331
	2/21	19,300	6/26	14,331	10/23	
	2/27	19,940	7/ 3	15,132	10/30	26,612
	3/ 6	19,525	7/10	15,834	11/ 6	27,793
	3/13	19,220	7/17	14,875	11/13	28,292
	3/20	19,578	7/24	14,965	11/20	38,702
	3/27	20,173	7/31	15,500	11/27	28,992
	4/ 3	11,470	8/ 7	16,101	12/ 4	31,991
	4/10	11,545	8/14	16,891		
	4/17	20,245	8/21	17,111		

1976 TOTAL MILES PER REPORTS: 19,148

GRAND TOTAL 38,928

ACTUAL MILEAGE 44,980

TO: ▮▮▮▮▮▮▮

In reply to your letter dated December 8, 1976 questioning my
mileage. I have never made a practice of recording my vacation
or extended weekend trips mileage on my expense report. I
consider this mileage is of a personal nature, and has no reflec
ion in reference to my company business. The ▮▮▮▮▮▮▮▮▮▮
District Manager Manual or any other written mandate has stated
that it is mandatory that personal and business mileage must
be recorded on a combined bases. Nor that mileage must be
recorded on a consecutive or concurrent bases, and has to
coincide with your odometer. I do subtract my five day week
personal mileage from my expense recorded mileage.

I could understand your concern if this situation was reversed
and that my odometer reflected less mileage than appeared on my
expense report. To clearify another question that was presented
in your letter there were variation in mileage that appeared fror
week to week on occasion, this is the result of my employing my
second car in work, plus on occasion I was forced to to use a
loaner while my car was being repaired. !If you are questioning
my intergity, I request a council amoung all partys concerned.

actual Mileage 44980

1975
4-5	69,452	11-1	13,412			
4-12	841	11-8	14,112		6-5	11,605
4-19	1,497	11-15	13,540		6-12	12,781
4-26	2,180	11-22	14,240		6-19	13,331
5-3	2,467	11-29			6-26	14,331
5-10	3,195	12-6	15,290		7-3	15,132
5-17	3,688	12-13	16,052		7-10	15,834
5-24	3,708	12-20	16,632		7-17	14,875
5-31	4,147	12-27	16,732		7-24	14,965
6-7	4,217	— 1976 —			7-31	15,500
6-14	4,572	1-3	16,782		8-7	16,101
6-21	4,884	1-10	17,342		8-14	16,891
6-28	5,491	1-17	17,980		8-21	17,111
7-5	6,051	1-24	15,240		8-28	
7-12	6,672	1-31	18,650		9-4	
7-19	7,328	2-7	13,730		9-11	17,041
		2-14	17,180		9-18	17,671
8-2	7,423	2-21	17,300		9-25	17,871
8-9	7,963	2-27	17,940			
8-16	5,943	3-6	17,525		10-9	24,794
8-23	6,684	3-13	17,220		10-16	25,331
8-30	7,376	3-20	17,578		10-23	26,056
9-6	7,776	3-27	20,173		10-30	26,612
9-13	8,676	4-3	11,470		11-6	27,743
9-20	8,536	4-10	11,545		11-13	28,292
9-27	10,135	4-17	20,245		11-20	38,782
10-4	10,816	4-24	20,223		11-27	28,972
10-11	11,485	5-1	20,273			
10-18	12,276	5-8	11,315			
10-25	12,576	5-22	11,480			

Mileage reported

████████████████████████

1/24/76   18240

5/8/76   11,248

8/21/76   17,111
9/11/76   17,041
11/13/76   25,292

11/20/76   38 78 2

11/27/76   28 992

Current Mileage
44900

MR. ██████████████

WE STATED ON TWO OCCASIONS THAT WE SEE LITTLE OR
NO NEED FOR YOUR VISITING THE ████████ PLANT EXCEPT
ON RARE OCCASIONS WHERE THIS OFFICE GIVES YOU DI-
RECTION, OR POSSIBLY, TO DISCUSS PROBLEMS WITH I.P.

WE FEEL VISITS TO I.P. ARE NOT NECESSARY BECAUSE
YOUR CONTACTS SHOULD BE MADE OVER THE PHONE FROM
A WHOLESALER LOCATION.

ADDITIONALLY, WE SUGGESTED TWICE THAT IF YOU HAVE
A NEED TO USE A COPY MACHINE, THAT YOUR NEEDS CAN
AND SHOULD BE SATISFIED BY USE OF THE DIVISION
OFFICE XEROX.

THIS IS A FINAL REQUEST THAT ALL COPYING WHEN YOU
ARE IN THE COLUMBUS MARKET BE DONE IN THE DIVISION
OFFICE FROM THIS DATE FORWARD WITH NO EXCEPTIONS,
TO REDUCE THE COST OF USING TWO COPY MACHINES. DO
NOT USE THE ████████ PLANT COPY MACHINE WITHOUT
PRIOR APPROVAL FROM THIS OFFICE.

ATTACHED FOR YOUR INFORMATION IS THE LATEST LIST OF
CHARGES TO THE DIVISION FOR YOUR USE OF THE COPY
MACHINE IN THE ████████ PLANT FOR APRIL. AS YOU
WILL RECALL, WE REQUESTED THAT YOU CEASE USING
THEIR MACHINE AS OF THE END OF MARCH.

CC: ████████████████

XEROX — AUDITRON READINGS

		DIVISION SALES		CENTRAL ENGINEERING				
		READING	USAGE	READING	USAGE			
12/76	METER	44868		7740				
1/77	METER	44868		7769				
	Jan. Usage				29			
2-77	METER	44988		7806				
	FEB Usage		120		37			
3-77	METER	44935		7852				
	MARCH Usage		020		46			
4-77	METER	45139		8464				
	APRIL Usage		201		612			
	Div							
	201 @ .02388 =	480						
	91 @ .02381 =	217						
	div 25 (66)	687						
	...(25)							
	Central Eng							
	612 @ .02388 =	1461						

EXHIBITS E CONT.

Please note Mr. ██████ letter dated May 6, 1977, in
which he states, "Attached for your information is the latest list
of charges to the Division for your use of the copy machine in
the ██████ Plant for April." This accusation is entirely
erroneous since to activate the ████████████ copy machine,
it is necessary to use a key or accutron counter, which was kept
in the Division office. Secondly, I was out of town on special
assignment those three weeks in April of 1977.

The only time I went to the ████████████ was to
deliver a consumer compaint open package (see illustration) or to
correct I.P. shipping problems. I also questioned ████████████
of the ████████████ Accounting Department to see if he had
approached ██████ in reference to my use of the copy machine.
██████ emphatically denied ever contacting ██████ with
regard to this matter.

Certainly it's obvious to me that Titus Marlowe would want to avoid the hostility of the division office, and go to the plant two blocks away to utilize their copier. I think I would have paid out of pocket at the neighborhood post office, library, drug store, wherever, to make copies, no matter the cost! Here was clear evidence of how Bruno Pittman orchestrated devious plans and manipuated people to harass or victimize company employees at his discretion. Those he felt should be terminated from the company were systematically harassed.

It's certainly not for me to evaluate Titus Marlowe's mental state, but with the burden of the preceding vacation questioned, the car mileage questioned, coupled with constantly having to defend your every action to managers throughout the hierarchy of The Company, what could have been his state? Finally, Titus Marlowe requested a transfer (Exhibit K) but the insensitive managers at the headquarters would not grant him a reprieve from Bruno Pittman's tyranny!

On June 13, 1977, Titus Marlowe was fired from The Company after fourteen and a half years of exemplary employment!

AT APPROXIMATELY 10:20 A.M. ON THE ABOVE DATE, ████████
███████ REPORTED TO THIS OFFICE AS INSTRUCTED.

WITH ME IN THE OFFICE WAS ████████████ WHO WOULD
BE AN OBSERVOR AND WITNESS TO THE FOLLOWING MEETING:

████████ WAS INFORMED BY ME THAT WE HAD CONCRETE
DOCUMENTATION THAT HE HAD VIOLATED THE TERMS OF HIS
PROBATION PERIOD AND THAT SINCE ████████████
HAD COPIED THE REGION OFFICE WITH AN ACCUSING LETTER,
MANAGEMENT HAD MADE THE DECISION TO TERMINATE HIS
EMPLOYMENT EFFECTIVE TODAY.

AT THAT TIME ████████ ACKNOWLEDGED AFFIRMATIVELY AND
SAID HE WOULD TAKE THIS MATTER TO COURT. HE THEN
STATED THAT I WAS WRONG AND THAT I WAS ON AN EGO
TRIP AND HE FELT IT COULD BE A RACIAL PROBLEM. HE
SEEMED TO BE IN AN ARGUMENTATIVE MOOD AND ACTED
VERY NERVOUSLY.

HE INDICATED THAT HE HAD PHONED ████████████ THIS
MORNING AND THAT ████████████ WOULD BE REQUESTING A
TRANSFER AND THAT OTHER DIVISION FIELD PERSONNEL
WERE DISENCHANTED WITH THE WORKINGS OF THE DIVISION
SINCE I HAD BECOME DIVISION MANAGER.

WE DID NOT ATTEMPT TO ANSWER HIS CHARGES BECAUSE
WE DID NOT WANT TO CREATE OR LEAD TO ANY HOSTILE
OR UNPLEASANT SITUATIONS HERE IN THIS OFFICE.

WE INFORMED ████████ THAT WE WOULD SEND ████████████
HOME WITH HIM TO PICK UP ALL DISTRICT RECORDS AND
COMPANY ISSUED EQUIPMENT. ████████ STATED THAT HE
WOULD TURN IN THE EQUIPMENT ON THURSDAY. WE AGAIN
REQUESTED THE SUBMISSION OF RECORDS AND EQUIPMENT
AND ████████ INFORMED ME THAT HE WAS GOING TO ████████
TO ATTEND HIS DAUGHTER'S GRADUATION AND HE WOULD
NOT TURN IN THE RECORDS AND EQUIPMENT UNTIL THURS-
DAY, JUNE 16.

████████████

PAGE 2

████████ ATTEMPTED AGAIN TO BECOME ARGUMENTATIVE, AT WHICH TIME I INFORMED HIM THAT WE WOULD CLOSE THE CONVERSATION AND HE WAS FREE TO LEAVE. HE SAID I HAD BEEN OUT TO GET HIM SINCE THE POST CONVENTION MEETING HERE IN COLUMBUS IN OCTOBER. HE THEN TURNED TO ████████████ TO VERIFY HIS FEELINGS DUE TO THE SITUATION WHICH HAS BEEN COVERED IN AN EARLIER MEMO TO FILE.

████████ THEN WAS INFORMED THAT SEVERANCE AND VACATION PAY WOULD BE APPROVED AFTER HE HAD SATISFIED HIS OBLIGATION TO RETURN TO THIS OFFICE ALL ██████ ASSIGNED EQUIPMENT AND WHOLESALER RECORDS. ████████ ACKNOWLEDGED AND LEFT THE OFFICE.

████████ RETURNED TO THE OFFICE LESS THAN A MINUTE LATER AND ASKED ME HOW HIS RETIREMENT BENEFITS WOULD BE HANDLED. MY REPLY WAS THAT I DID NOT KNOW BUT WOULD FIND OUT FOR HIM FROM ████████ AND PASS THE INFORMATION ON TO HIM AS SOON AS WE KNEW.

EMPLOYEE SALARY STATUS REVIEW

EFFECTIVE

☐ Annual   ☑ Original Six Months   ☐ Six Months After Promotion

NAME	EMP. NO.	ST. NO	CODE	SEP. DATE	PRESENT MONTHLY SALARY
	B3454	04	TM029		400 00

POSITION TITLE	DATE EMP.	W & H	GRADE	RECOMMENDED INCREASE
Trainee - Merchandising and Sales Promoter (Gr. 070)	11 62	2	061	30 00

NEW MONTHLY SALARY: 430 00

Job performance should be carefully considered and recommendation for an increase should be based strictly on the meritorious performance of the employee.

An increase at this time is ☑ is not ☐ recommended because: this man is doing a good job in all phases of merchandising. Follows through very carefully on any given assignment by the Branch Manager and Merchandising Supervisor. His work has always given evidence of his effort to succeed with our Company. Increase is well merited.

ADDITIONAL EDUCATION

NAME OF SCHOOL OR UNIVERSITY	DATES ATTENDED FROM	TO	DEGREE OR CERTIFICATE RECEIVED OR NAME OF COURSE COMPLETED

ADMINISTRATIVE COMMITTEE

VISION HEAD

SALARY ADMINISTRATOR

Turn original and two copies to the Salary Administrator through channels prior to the 20th of the month.

EMPLOYEE SALARY STATUS REVIEW

EFFECTIVE

☐ Annual ☐ Original Six Months ☒ Six Months After Promotion partial
adjustment to grade minimum

NAME	EMP. NO. B-3454	GR. NO. 9-4	CODE TM-029	RV DATE 6	63	PRESENT MONTHLY SALARY 445 00
POSITION TITLE Trainee- Merchandising & Sales Promoter (Gr. 7)			DATE EMP. 11	W & H 62	GRADE 061	RECOMMENDED INCREASE 25 00
						NEW MONTHLY SALARY 470 00

Job performance should be carefully considered and recommendation for an increase should be based strictly on the meritorious performance of the employee.

An increase at this time is ☒ is not ☐ recommended because: he has just completed his first full year as a Merchandising Sales Trainee and has performed his duties in creditable manner and is a valuable asset to our Negro market. He has been given additional assignments in sales territorial work, special [redacted] promotion, new tab top introduction and as a sp_____ representative at conventions and shows. All these assignments have been carried out with commendable satisfactory results. Financial conditions permitting, he expects to complete the 14 hours necessary for a master's degree in education. We rate him a very good potential for future promotion.

He sacrificed over $100.00 a month income in making the transition from his previous employment to this opportunity for a sales career.

ADDITIONAL EDUCATION

NAME OF SCHOOL OR UNIVERSITY	DATES ATTENDED		DEGREE OR CERTIFICATE RECEIVED OR NAME OF COURSE COMPLETED
	FROM	TO	

ADMINISTRATIVE COMMITTEE

DIVISION HEAD

SALARY ADMINISTRATOR

Return original and two copies to the Salary Administrator through channels prior to the 20th of the month.

Dear ██████

It is a real pleasure to advise you that the Salary Committee has approved the joint recommendation of the Sales Manager of our Region and myself that you be granted an increase in salary of $25.00 per month effective November 1, 1963.

I am sure you appreciate that this additional income carries with it additional responsibility and I am looking forward to your continuing to give the industrious, efficient and loyal service that merited this increase.

Sincerely,

EMPLOYEE SALARY STATUS REVIEW

EFFECTIVE

SIX MONTHS AFTER PROMOTION

NAME	EMP NO.	GR. NO	CODE	EFF. DATE	PRESENT MONTHLY SALARY
	B3454	04	13-029-00	11-63	470.00
POSITION TITLE	DATE EMP	W & M	GRADE		RECOMMENDED INCREASE
MERCHANDISING AND SALES PROMOTER - Trainee	11-62	2	06-1		25 00
					NEW MONTHLY SALARY
					495 00

Job performance should be carefully considered and recommendation for an increase should be based strictly on the meritorious performance of the employee.

An increase at this time is [X] is not [ ] recommended because: he is capable, conscientious and thorough

in his duties of merchandising and promotional work, sales territory assignments

and other special promotional activities in our large Negro territory. He

sacrificed over $75.00 a month income to take advantage of the opportunity to make

a career in sales and by his past performance has proven to possess the qualifica-

tions for future promotions with our fine Company. We believe an increase in

salary at this time is well merited.

ADDITIONAL EDUCATION

NAME OF SCHOOL OR UNIVERSITY	DATES ATTENDED		DEGREE OR CERTIFICATE RECEIVED OR NAME OF COURSE COMPLETED
	FROM	TO	

Job performance and job specification have been reviewed with

ADMINISTRATIVE COMMITTEE

DEPARTMENT HEAD

DIVISION HEAD

SALARY ADMINISTRATOR

Return original and two copies to the Salary Administrator through approved channels within 10 days

EMPLOYEE SALARY STATUS REVIEW

EFFECTIVE

SIX MONTHS AFTER PROMOTION

NAME	EMP. NO.	GR. NO.	CODE	EFF. DATE	PRESENT MONTHLY SALARY
	B3454	Q3	13-029-00	06-64	510.00

POSITION TITLE	DATE EMP. [W & M]	GRADE	RECOMMENDED INCREASE
MERCHANDISING AND SALES PROMOTER	11-62	2	06-1	25.00

NEW MONTHLY SALARY

535.00

Job performance should be carefully considered and recommendation for an increase should be based strictly on the meritorious performance of the employee.

An increase at this time is ☒ is not ☐ recommended because: since his transfer from the Chicago-South Branc

he is still learning the many functions and responsibilities of his new and important

assignment in our negro territory. His merchandising and display work has been good.

He is a very hard worker and is never reluctant to tackle special assignments. With

further training I am confident he will be promotable to a sales territory in the near

future.

ADDITIONAL EDUCATION

NAME OF SCHOOL OR UNIVERSITY	DATES ATTENDED FROM	TO	DEGREE OR CERTIFICATE RECEIVED OR NAME OF COURSE COMPLETED
None			

Job performance and job specification have been reviewed with the subject employee. Yes ☒ No ☐ . If present job specification is not properly descriptive of job requirements, please attach revised job description or memorandum to amend.

ADMINISTRATIVE COMMITTEE

DIVISION HEAD

SALARY ADMINISTRATOR

Return original and two copies to the Salary Administrator through channels prior to the 20th of the month.

EMPLOYEE SALARY STATUS REVIEW

EFFECTIVE _____

ANNUAL

NAME			EMP. NO.	GR. NO.	CODE		EFF. DATE	PRESENT MONTHLY SALARY
			63454	Q5	15-025-00		11-64	325.00
POSITION TITLE			DATE EMP.	W 3 H	GRADE			RECOMMENDED INCREASE
MERCHANDISING AND SALES PROMOTER			11-62	.	Q 7-6			20.00
								NEW MONTHLY SALARY
								$75.00

Job performance should be carefully considered and recommendation for an increase should be based strictly on the meritorious performance of the employee.

An increase at this time is ☒ is not ☐ recommended because: of the fine progress he has made in our Negro territory. As a merchandiser and sales promoter he has done a commendable job. He is well liked by his retailers and by his co-workers. He is a willing worker and his personal habits are good. I am sure he has only scratched the surface of his potential and when placed as a salesman trainee that he will satisfy our needs.

ADDITIONAL EDUCATION

NAME OF SCHOOL OR UNIVERSITY	DATES ATTENDED FROM	TO	DEGREE OR CERTIFICATE RECEIVED OR NAME OF COURSE COMPLETED
None			

Job performance and job specification have been reviewed with the subject employee. Yes ☒ No ☐ . If present job specification is not properly descriptive of job requirements, please attach revised job description or memorandum to amend.

ADMINISTRATIVE COMMITTEE

SUPERVISOR

DEPARTMENT HEAD

DIVISION HEAD

SALARY ADMINISTRATOR

Return original and two copies to the Salary Administrator through channel.

SIX MONTHS AFTER PROMOTION

NAME	EMP. NO.	GR. NO.	CODE	EFF. DATE	PRESENT MONTHLY SALARY
▓▓▓▓	83454	03	19-013-00	07-65	585.00

POSITION TITLE	DATE EMP.	W S H	GRADE	RECOMMENDED INCREASE
SALESMAN, BEER BRANCH	11-62	7	08-0	20.00

NEW MONTHLY SALARY
605.00

Job performance should be carefully considered and recommendation for an increase should be based strictly on the meritorious performance of the employee.

An increase at this time is ☒ is not ☐ recommended because: his territory is showing a total R/E increase of 13% for the first ten months of this year. In November, he acquired 100 new items, 34 being ▓▓▓▓ in Bottles. He has 274 accounts with a 4.8 multiple distribution factor which is above branch level. His bookings and placing of P.O.S. is very good. He is well liked by his retailers and gets their cooperation in many store promotions. His personal habits are very good.

ADDITIONAL EDUCATION

NAME OF SCHOOL OR UNIVERSITY	DATES ATTENDED FROM	TO	DEGREE OR CERTIFICATE RECEIVED OR NAME OF COURSE COMPLETED
None			

Job performance and job specification have been reviewed with the subject employee. Yes ☒ No ☐ . If present job specification is not properly descriptive of job requirements, please attach revised job description or memorandum to amend.

ADMINISTRATIVE COMMITTEE

SUPERVISOR

DEPARTMENT HEAD

DIVISION HEAD

SALARY ADMINISTRATOR

Return original and two copies to the Salary Administrator through channels arriving on the 25th of the month

ANNUAL

NAME	EMP. NO.	GR. NO.	CODE	EFF. DATE	PRESENT MONTHLY SALARY
▮▮▮▮▮▮▮	83454	03	19-013-00	01-66	600.00
POSITION TITLE			DATE EMP.	W & M	GRADE	RECOMMENDED INCREASE
SALESMAN, BEER BRANCH			11-62	2	08-0	15.00
					NEW MONTHLY SALARY	615.00

Job performance should be carefully considered and recommendation for an increase should be based strictly on the meritorious performance of the employee:

An increase at this time is ☒ is not ☐ recommended because: his territory had a 13% B.E. increase in 1965 and continues to show the same trend for the first two months of this year.

He placed 41 new items in January and 49 in February. He maintains an accurate set of route books. Regional Representative, ▮▮▮▮▮▮, worked with this salesman January 24-28, 1966 and reported that he was impressed with his over-all performance. His immediate supervisor concurs with this.

ADDITIONAL EDUCATION

NAME OF SCHOOL OR UNIVERSITY	DATES ATTENDED		DEGREE OR CERTIFICATE RECEIVED OR NAME OF COURSE COMPLETED
	FROM	TO	
None			

Job performance and job specification have been reviewed with the subject employee. Yes ☒ No ☐. If present job specification is not properly descriptive of job requirements, please attach revised job description or memorandum to amend.

ADMINISTRATIVE COMMITTEE

▮▮▮▮▮▮▮▮▮▮

SUPERVISOR

DEPARTMENT HEAD

DIVISION HEAD

SALARY ADMINISTRATOR

ANNUAL

NAME			EMP. NO.	GR. NO.	CODE	EFF. DATE	PRESENT MONTHLY SALARY
████████			83454	04	19-013-00	05-66	615.00
POSITION TITLE SALESMAN, BEER BRANCH			DATE EMP. 11-62	W & H 2	GRADE 08-0	RECOMMENDED INCREASE	25.00
						NEW MONTHLY SALARY	640.00

Job performance should be carefully considered and recommendation for an increase should be based strictly on the meritorious performance of the employee.

An increase at this time is ☒ is not ☐ recommended because: __He continues to do a consistently good job in managing his sales territory. His over-all performance is very good in securing new accounts, P.O.S. and new package placements. He is a good worker and constantly strives to increase sales in his territory. He has a good knowledge of all company policies and procedures. His personal habits are good and is well liked by retailers and fellow workers. He is well qualified in the position he holds.

ADDITIONAL EDUCATION

NAME OF SCHOOL OR UNIVERSITY	DATES ATTENDED		DEGREE OR CERTIFICATE RECEIVED OR NAME OF COURSE COMPLETED
	FROM	TO	

Job performance and job specification have been reviewed with

ADMINISTRATIVE COMMITTEE

SALARY ADMINISTRATOR

Return original and two copies to the Salary Administrator through channels prior to the 20th of the month.

Dear

I have been advised that you celebrate your
fifth anniversary with our Company this month.

Please accept my congratulations on your length
of service with our fine Company, and your futur
loyalty and sincere efforts will be very much
appreciated by me personally.

Kind regards and best wishes.

Sincerely,

Dear ▮▮▮▮

Congratulations on being nominated to the ▮▮▮▮▮ All American Sales Society. Your Branch Manager has recommended you based on your consistently fine performance not only during the month of August but in previous months.

Would appreciate your forwarding to this office your home address, city and state, and your sports coat size. As soon as we have received this information we will forward it to ▮▮▮▮▮ and they in turn will send you a distinctive ▮▮▮▮▮ Blazer which signifies your membership in this prestigious society.

Once again, our congratulations on your fine performance.

Sincerely,

Division Manager

cc: Messrs. ▮▮▮▮▮

APPRAISAL

NAME	EMP. NO.	GR. NO.	CODE	EFF. DATE	PRESENT MONTHLY SALARY
▮▮▮▮▮▮▮▮	R3454	04	19-013-00	05-67	640.00
POSITION TITLE			DATE EMP.	WEN	GRADE	RECOMMENDED INCREASE
SALESMAN, 2ㄴYR BRANCH			11-62	2	08-0	25.00
					NEW MONTHLY SALARY
					665.00

Job performance should be carefully considered and recommendation for an increase should be based strictly on the meritorious performance of the employee.

An increase at this time is [XX] is not [ ] recommended because: Of his diligent work on the North
and West side, his efforts were responsible for this area showing an
increase of 21,564 s/c in 1967. He has been transferred to a new territory
since January, 1968, and I am positive that his over-all performance will
enable this area to become as productive as the one he recently relinquished.
He was a recipient of the ▮▮▮▮▮ All American Sales Society Blazer in 1967,
and he has consistently given a fine performance. His over-all performance
is to be commended. He carries out all assignments to the fullest.

ADDITIONAL EDUCATION

NAME OF SCHOOL OR UNIVERSITY	DATES ATTENDED FROM	TO	DEGREE OR CERTIFICATE RECEIVED OR NAME OF COURSE COMPLETED

Job performance and job specification have been reviewed with the subject employee. Yes [XX] No [ ] . If present job specification is not properly descriptive of job requirements, please attach revised job description or memorandum to amend.

ADMINISTRATIVE COMMITTEE

SUPERVISOR

SALARY ADMINISTRATOR

EMPLOYEE SALARY STATUS REVIEW

EFFECTIVE _____

SIX MONTHS AFTER PROMOTION

	EMP. NO	GR. NO	CODE	EFF. DATE	PRESENT MONTHLY SALARY
	83454	Q4	01-225-00	07-68	715.00
PERSON TITLE		DATE EMP.	W&H	GRADE	RECOMMENDED INCREASE
ASSISTANT ROUTE SUPERVISOR		11-62	2	08-1	25.00
				NEW MONTHLY SALARY	740.00

 # performance should be carefully considered and recommendation for an increase should be based strictly on the meritorious performance
 # the employee.

 # increase at this time is [XX] *is not* [ ] *recommended because:* __He has progressed very well in the__
__performance of his duties in the newly created position. He is capable__
__and enthusiastic in carrying out all assignments. He is very thorough,__
__willing to learn and to apply his knowledge to his position. Both his__
__attitude and ability tend to make him a valuable asset to the Route__
__Supervisor Department.__

ADDITIONAL EDUCATION

NAME OF SCHOOL OR UNIVERSITY	DATES ATTENDED		DEGREE OR CERTIFICATE RECEIVED OR NAME OF COURSE COMPLETED
	FROM	TO	

Job performance and job specification have been reviewed with the subject employee. Yes [XX] *No* [ ] *. If present job specification is not properly descriptive of job requirements, please attach revised job description or memorandum to amend.*

ADMINISTRATIVE COMMITTEE

APPROVED

DIVISION HEAD

SALARY ADMINISTRATOR

Return original and two copies to the Salary Administrator through channels prior to the 20th of the month

EMPLOYEE SALARY STATUS REVIEW

EFFECTIVE _____

SIX MONTHS AFTER PROMOTION

NAME	EMP NO	GR. NO.	CODE	EFF. DATE	PRESENT MONTHLY SALARY
	B3454	04	01-225-00	01-69	740.00

POSITION TITLE	DATE EMP.	W & H	GRADE	RECOMMENDED INCREASE
ASSISTANT ROUTE SUPERVISOR	11-62	2	08-1	40.00

NEW MONTHLY SALARY
780.00

Job performance should be carefully considered and recommendation for an increase should be based strictly on the meritorious performance of the employee.

An increase at this time is XXX is not [ ] recommended because: . He continues to do a consistently good
job in the performance of his duties. He is enthusiastic and very diligent
in carrying out all assignments. He has both the attitude and ability to
accept added responsibility in the future.

ADDITIONAL EDUCATION

NAME OF SCHOOL OR UNIVERSITY	DATES ATTENDED		DEGREE OR CERTIFICATE RECEIVED OR NAME OF COURSE COMPLETED
	FROM	TO	

Job performance and job specification have been reviewed with the subject employee. Yes XXX No [ ] . If present job specification is not properly descriptive of job requirements, please attach revised job description or memorandum to amend.

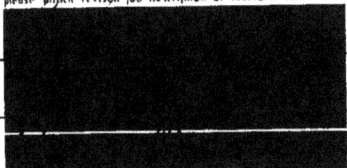

ADMINISTRATIVE COMMITTEE

APPROVED

JUL 11 1969

DIVISION HEAD

SALARY ADMINISTRATOR

Return original and two copies to the Salary Administrator through channels prior to the 20th of the month.

The Confrontation 6

The Pennsylvania Business School, Wharton, conducted an in-depth comprehensive time and motion study of field managers. They concluded that the average time field managers worked was 68 hours per week. (Little wonder Titus Marlowe had problems.) It was because of this study and recommendation that typist such as Helen Barken were authorized. To supplement this effort, field managers were issued Lanier pocket tape recorders. The theory was that field marketing managers would record their reports on tape, send them to the secretary for typing, then she/he would send the typed reports back to the Manager for proofing and approval.

Of course, all of this was to happen in just a few days turn-around time. With the creation of my new district and the appointment sometime in the future of my replacement, Helen Barken would have five field managers to type for and she was also to assist Bruno Pittman's secretary, Lynn Thaxton.

On June 1, 1979, District XXX came into existence with its very reluctant District Manager, armed with the knowledge that Titus Marlowe was indeed fired as a result of a letter from a wholesaler. The wholesalers in my new district eagerly awaited my assignment. The Vice President at the largest wholesalers in my District welcomed me by putting a Black Cabbage Patch doll on the shelf in his office for all employees to see! At the very onset I was wondering what kind of files were being kept on me. I was conscious of my every move, even how long I stayed in the bathroom. The sales office was adjacent to the Vice President's, the office door was always open and the partition was glass, the sales force and others would look at the doll and then kind of smile at me. Of all the employees in my district of northwest Ohio, there was only one Black, a part-time driver, even if I had attended a training program things would have been tough! This time I knew The Company policy regarding relocation. I had three months before Bruno Pittman would have to file an extension. Three months to decide what to do, to find another job, to move back to Chicago, to California, to buy a car.

During my tenure in the Region Office, I would visit my parents in the evening. One day my mother told me that my father's car had simply died. My father, who had never owned a new car, was trying to send his last child through dental school and could not afford to buy a new car. My father was almost over the hump. He had sent four children off to college, away from the gangs and violence of Chicago, and without any assistance was now trying to help his youngest fulfill his dream of becoming a dentist. All this from a man who had no formal education. I told my mother he would be doing me a favor if he took over my car payments, he could have my car and pay me when he could.

During the month of June, I would visit the new district. It took some getting use to traveling rural single lane highways through the cornfields. There were no large interstate signs alerting you that your exit was coming up in one or two miles, instead you would come to a stop sign and the different rural route signs would point what direction to take; there was no automobile club here. It also took some getting use to, seeing all the pickup trucks with rebel flags attached all over the vehicle.

Helen was very helpful in getting me organized with all the new reports I was encountering. There was so much; each of the District Managers that my district had been developed from just dumped their files on me. I did not inherit the structure of a previous district, and I never could have gotten off of first base without Helen. She was very enthusiastic about working at The Company and was a happy person for everyone to be around. One day Helen told me that her daughter Mary, age 12, had been diagnosed with scoliosis of the spine and that she was concerned with upcoming medical expenses. Bruno would call the District Managers to Columbus almost every other week, and just about every evening, Lynn would call her girlfriends and everyone would go dancing and drinking.

Louis Scott was promoted to District Representative from Illinois, College Representative in May of 1979. Louie, as he liked to be called, was a graduate of Ball State University, Indiana. Louie, unlike most of the other staff, was still young at heart, unbiased, and somewhat like myself, trusting and naive to the workings of big business and Bruno Pittman. Louie also was soon indoctrinated to the drinking and partying that was paramount. In retrospect, I often wonder how many lives have been changed by a whole range of problems associated with alcohol abuse, date rape, unwanted pregnancies and abortions, drunken driving, introduction to drugs, and for some, a lifetime of alcoholism.

It was the fall and business was chaotic, field managers were besieged with requests from St. Louis for financial commitments from wholesalers. The Company was also asking the wholesalers to outlay a huge capital expense in insulating and ventilating the warehouses. Sales of The Company products were poor and progressively getting worse, particularly Bratbrau. Miller seemed to be doing everything right and getting a jump on Brat at every juncture. The morale among wholesalers was very low, and there was a great deal of animosity towards Bruno Pittman. During sit-down luncheons, field managers were not allowed to sit at the tables with the wholesalers and their personnel. It was always the duty of the lowest man on the echelon to go into the dining room before meals and tilt the chair onto the table. This was the signal to wholesalers that this table was taken. However, when the field managers were in their respective districts, it was standard operating procedure to eat with the wholesalers and their personnel.

Mental Collapse

Today there is a lot of information and resources concerning "job stress." I was physically fatigued from relocation, traveling, learning a new job on my own, and totally exhausted mentally. My thirteen months with The Company had been one situation after another and there was no one in The Company to turn to. The NCRF was a great deal of solace through all of this; however, there should have been an area of recourse at The Company headquarters. They were obviously insensitive to the plight of their employees. The NCRF was my future legal recourse, but they were not professional counselors. I would not realize until years later, but I was now showing signs of "stress syndrome."

James Bond 007

It was at this point that I purchased telephone recording equipment. Bratbrau, Leafbrau, what's that, we were hardly concerned with Sales, it was covert activity against Jews, Blacks, and women. I also purchased devices to detect if my telephone conversations were being recorded. This was the cold war, all right. I pretended to be looking for a house to purchase in Toledo, the reason for my delay in moving. I didn't want to put down any roots, working in this kind of environment. I wanted to be free to move to another city on short notice. What a surprise, The Company would call me into court to testify for the defense, and voila, I would turn out to be the big witness, tapes and all for the claimant! I didn't know at the time that I was laying the cornerstone for a book. Another noteworthy point—that summer was the hiring of my replacement Victor Turner. At the first opportunity, I told Victor that he was working for the modern version of "Hitler" and about Bruno's track record with minorities.

In August 1979 the District Managers were sent employee evaluation forms for Helen's six-month performance review. The following week I made it a point to be out of town during Helen's review. It did not take Bruno long. He simply surprised Helen with typing errors circled in red and gave her the choice of resigning or being fired and having that on her record. Feeling intimidated, insecure, and frightened, Helen Barken resigned from The Company, Inc.

That weekend there was a knock at my door. Much to my chagrin, it was Helen. Her daughters were downstairs in the parking lot standing next to her car. I went out on the porch to talk with her. Helen, with tears in her eyes, proceeded to tell me about what had transpired during her performance review. As she was talking, I was looking at her daughters, Heather, age 10 and Mary, age 12, now wearing that God-awful, hideous body brace to remedy the scoliosis.

I guess they knew that there was something wrong. I remember the sadness on their faces. I could not look at Helen as she told me that this was unexpected, that she thought she had done a pretty good job. She was so shocked at Bruno's abrasiveness, and sense of anger during her review. She was also at a loss to explain the typing errors, and perhaps the biggest shock of all, the District Managers' evaluation of her work. Helen spoke of how she thought everyone in the division office was her friend including Bruno—the many nights of going out laughing, drinking and partying. My eyes stayed focused in the direction of the girls as she spoke. I wondered about her financial situation, which certainly had to be compounded with Mary's medical problem. I wasn't sure if a potential employer might not view Mary's scoliosis as a major medical expense, and thus not hire Helen. My anxiety level was just so high. Here was a genuine person, a single mother, crying on my porch with her daughters looking very sad, one in a virtual body brace, not knowing why she was fired, facing an unknown future. I went back into the apartment and grabbed tissue for Helen's tears. By now Helen was explaining how much she enjoyed working for The Company and the division office personnel. She spoke of the good times we had drinking and dancing, she laughed about all the morning hangovers. If she only knew that the partying or the lack thereof was the cause of her demise!

What had Helen done to bring Bruno's wrath upon her? Helen went to Bruno after a few months of the drinking and partying sessions and confided that she felt she was being unfair to her children. Bruno responded that he and/or we would pay for a babysitter when the District Managers were in town. To Helen, the point was that she had an obligation to spend quality time with her daughters. That afternoon I assured Helen that a person of her caliber and personality would not have a problem finding a position. As a job reference, I would be only too glad to give her a recommendation. I also told her not to hesitate in calling if she or the girls needed anything.

Finally, it was Helen's turn to confide. She told me that shortly after she started work, she was informed that Bruno was a racist and to be careful not to appear to be too close, friendly, or helpful to me. I can vividly remember Helen looking me in the eye and squeezing my hand, saying, "watch Bruno." There was a sense of sadness as she and the girls got into the car. As the car drove away, they each waved good-bye to their FRIEND!

I had only been employed by The Company thirteen months but the strain was starting to show. The weekend flights to Chicago, the two-hour bus ride from Chicago's O'Hare Airport, usually getting home between 8 and 9 p.m. The unpacking, the usual Saturday activities—cleaners, hair-cut, banking, paying bills, the administrative work, repacking, the bus trip to the airport and back to Columbus all by 8 a.m. Monday. Learning the geography of Ohio, and the thirteen wholesalers and their personnel located throughout the state, learning the city's streets was an ordeal. Typing till 3 or 4 in the morning on 3-part carbon paper, the constant change in schedules, some-time two or three states in a week was all physically exhausting. All the late night drinking and the lack of exercise of any type were adding to the fatigue.

Then there was the mental stress. To finance all of the traveling, The Company issued travel letters but the limit was only $500. Many weeks my expense with airfares, lodging, and food exceeded that amount. My credit cards were just getting me by. I was doing a lot of manipulation between my savings and checking accounts. There were the little aggravations of having to go to the other side of town to East Columbus for a haircut and of course, there was a lot of trial and error, error, error, before I found a barber I could live with. There was the fact that I had to complete thirteen market reports between September and the end of the year and this did not exclude the weekly assignments which always seemed to be last minute. (I would find out later from Lynn concerning Louis Scott and the last minute game). There was the assignment to the region office, and then the promotion to a district in rural Ohio and the stress of not wanting to move to Toledo, Ohio. I had virtually taught myself the mannerisms of a businessman. I wore the suit, shoes, tie, even the wristwatch. All the social etiquette, the body language, the stance, all this was about to be wasted on rural Ohio. And as if this was not enough, there were the hidden agendas, the revelation of Bruno, the incident regarding Leo Sampson, the pending legal suit of Titus

Marlowe and my eventual role. The company's cold-blooded treatment of Jewish wholesalers, the remarks of putting Jews in a microwave oven, and lastly the demise of Helen Barken—all now taking their toll.

My girlfriend and I tried to maintain a long distance romance but my situation was just so tenuous, there was no time for cultivating a relationship. I hardly knew where I would be from week to week. There was no time or opportunity to have a life outside of The Company. I could not be on a bowling or softball team, Ohio State football had season sellouts. The legitimate theater, for which I had developed an insatiable appetite, virtually did not exist in Columbus and then I didn't even have a date to take. Traveling in my new district, there were virtually only farm reports on the car radio.

My feelings, my emotions were all pent up inside, there was no racquetball or tennis games for a release. There were only the four or five sessions with Titus Marlowe and the attorneys to tell what was happening within the structure of this major corporation. As an adult, I had not developed a close relationship with a minister who perhaps I could have confided in. In those days, there was little talk or acknowledgement of job stress and of how its affliction could manifest itself. There's the physical effect of head, neck and stomachaches and then there is the mental anguish and its associated symptoms. I could have quit had it not been for my father's letter. I was going through Army basic training during the winter of 1972 in Fort Leonardwood, Missouri. It was during the Vietnam conflict, so the training was six days a week in weather far below zero degrees. I was not contemplating AWOL (absent with out leave) but I certainly wasn't crazy about the situation I was in. Certainly not taking orders from men that I wasn't sure completed high school, and me, with the ink still wet on my bachelor's degree. Anyway, part of my father's letter said, "I did it, so can you."

A few weeks passed by, and I was busy as all get out and still debating what to do about moving. On Monday, Lynn called me in Toledo, Ohio to ask if I planned to follow my itinerary. I thought the question was a little out of the ordinary, but replied yes. On Tuesday, there were the same questions, but there were always changes in plans and call meetings, so again I was not too concerned with the questions. Wednesday morning, Lynn informed me that Bruno wanted to meet the first thing Thursday morning and that I should make the 120-mile drive back to Columbus that day.

The Conspiracy Continues

That evening, around 8:00 p.m., the phone rang; it was Bruno. He told me that he and I had a meeting in St. Louis Thursday morning. It would be a brief turn around meeting and I wouldn't need to pack clothes or even bring a briefcase. There was no need to make flight reservations, he already had the airline tickets. Again, I reflect on how naive I was then, and so trusting. That morning, as I was leaving the house, it was as if I was naked going somewhere without a briefcase. I grabbed my briefcase, legal pad and, by sheer coincidence, my Lanier tape recorder. In my mind, I thought a business person should carry a briefcase all of the time. That morning I met Bruno at the airport—on the plane, he never ever once mentioned our true reason for the trip.

We took a cab from the airport to World Headquarters. We received our visitors' passes from the receptionist when Bruno said, "Jim, let's take a seat before we go up, I want to talk." Bruno told me that I had been accused of rape and that I was going to be deposed by one of The Company's attorneys. Of course, I became totally discombobulated. We proceeded to a conference room in the legal department, where again I was surprised at the number of people in the room. There was Richard Stone, the Region Manager; his assistant, Ben Sinclair; James Hooks; Assistant to the Vice President of Sales; the attorneys, Bruno and myself.

Everyone greeted me with the usual formalities, we sat and I put the briefcase on my lap. The attorney explained why we were all here and proceeded to tell me that I was accused of molestation. At least this was a relief from the rape charge that Bruno had informed me I was accused of.

As the questioning began, I got the feeling of deja vu, Helen Barken's image appeared and I quickly pulled the Lanier recorder from the briefcase. Their eyes got as big as silver dollars and a look of panic came on their faces. I guess this was the last thing they counted on. I could see the pointed looks at Bruno, he had blown it, I was to have come totally unprepared.

The attorney quickly stated that the tape player was unnecessary and I replied that no one had informed me of these proceedings, and obviously everyone had known for some time of this meeting. The attorney again tried to assure me that the tape was not necessary and tried to enlist the support of his co-conspirators.

Now it was their turn to be intimidated, no one would utter a word with the tape player on. After a great deal of coaxing, I turned the player off, but after a few seconds I turned it back on. The attorney's tone and manner were now changed. He went from voraciousness and hostility to meekness and conciliation. There were no longer questions, simply statements. I was accused of touching a co-worker in my hotel room one night, and at the conclusion I was asked if I had anything to say. Of course, there was only the denial.

The attorney posed the questions to his co-conspirators, "Do you have any questions you would like to ask of Jim?" He was looking at them with a pleading look like, "Look, fellows, don't leave me out here hanging by myself." The entire group, much to my surprise, indicated no by shaking their heads. Not one man asked a question, or even answered no.

I knew then that fate had me put the recorder in the briefcase, now my dilemma was if they were going to let me get out of the building with the tape. I was asked to wait in the hall while they deliberated. A few moments later, Bruno came out and asked me to go into Bill Teller's office, the Vice President of Sales, and wait. As I sat in Bill's office, I looked at his awards and accolades. The more time I spent in the office, the angrier I got. What I really wanted to do was play the recording back, to hear the attorney from The Company mete out his statements, and to hear the silence of all those present in the room. I thought about how they might appear in Bill's office with security officers and demand the tape, and try to take it by force.

Bruno had the airline tickets for our return to Columbus. I thought I should just leave and purchase a ticket at the airport. It was just at this point that Bruno appeared, he gave me my ticket and told me to go ahead, he had to stay at the corporate office and would take a later flight. Just as well, I would not have been able to stand to sit next to him on the flight back.

I made a beeline out of that building, and once at the airport, you can guess who I called, another attorney. Mr. Leimert would be available when I got back to Columbus. By now, the delayed stress syndrome was being replaced with pure high octane adrenaline. Once in Mr. Leimert's office, I explained how the situation had come about and how by chance I had happened to bring along the tape player. After the tape had played, I guess I expected him to come over and slap me on the back, but I was in for another shock! Mr. Leimert pushed his chair back from his desk and proceeded to tell me how I blew it. He then proceeded to admonish me for not realizing what or who I was dealing with, for not dealing with this matter in a devious, cunning manner. What I should have done in the meeting was put the tape player back in the briefcase and then flicked it on, thereby giving them the sense of security so that their true identities and purpose would have revealed itself. So there it was, Bruno Pittman and The Company, against Jim Hobson, 007. There was no quitting, we were playing hard ball. I did not know this material would be a source for a book. I thought more in terms of litigation in a civil suit. I assured Mr. Leimert that in the future I would be cunning and cover my ass!

The next morning I walked into Bruno's office feeling confident. I stopped a few feet in front of his desk. Bruno jumped from his chair and literally ran towards me. I planted my feet, bent my knees and prepared to duck his first swing and counter with an uppercut to the jaw. Bruno stopped a few feet in front of me and stuck out his right hand with split second speed.

As we were shaking hands, he was smiling and saying how I had put one over on those bastards. How after I left he was admonished for letting me bring the tape player. He closed by saying that as far as he was concerned, the incident was over. It was becoming a tradition, each time I would have something incriminating on tape or on paper, I would go home and open a beer to toast myself. Cheers!

Life In A Fishbowl　7

runo's distinctive, red Delta 88 rode briskly by my apartment. It was September 1979, moving day. My apartment was located at the rear of a complex on a one way cul-de-sac separated by a boulevard. Once on the street, you came into my full view from my second-story porch. I was seated on the porch, reading mail, and attempting to stay out of the movers' way. Oh, yes, this time I had movers! I just happened to raise my eyes to see a car that was remarkably like Bruno's coming around the bend into full view.

Had Bruno come to help me move? Bruno's car did not pull off into the parking lot and as it passed by me, I could see a Black man in the passenger's seat. As the car exited the cul-de-sac, I could see Bruno glancing up at me. In the 35 to 45 seconds it took for this to happen, I never once moved my head from its downward position. I just followed them with my eyes. In subsequent conversations, neither Bruno or I mentioned the "drive-by."

I'm sure somewhere in the town there is a person that likes Toledo, Ohio. For me, Toledo was the armpit of Ohio and the rest of my district was lower down and to the rear of the human anatomy. This was a district and city totally devoid of Black culture, a blue-collar town in the middle of the rust bucket, it might as well been jump-back Mississippi. Out of the six wholesalers that comprised my district, there was one Black part-time employee in the whole quadrant of the state. There were no Black-formatted radio stations and when you went to the most prestigious department store, they would pullout the good old catalog to order the clothes and shoes you wanted and could receive in two to six weeks. In all fairness, I must add that if you weren't happy with the selection, they were more than happy to return the merchandise and repeat the process all over. I guess because the area only averaged 75 days of sunshine per year, and the economy was poor with few white collar jobs, most young Blacks with degrees, with the exception of you-know-who, left. One reason that was popular as to why Toledo never developed socially was that it was in close proximity to Detroit, Michigan, 45 miles, but for me it might as well been 445 miles (I will explain that one a little later.)

I moved into an inexpensive apartment complex on the edge of town. It was very cheap and I got a six month lease. I figured I wouldn't be there long. I only unpacked the necessities, there was no need to be formal. In the fourteen months I lived in Columbus I had visitors once, and I was sure that was going to be 100% more than Toledo.

With no formal training and the knowledge that I worked for a racist, and a company insensitive to Blacks, the rural wholesalers of District XXX were poised to make "hell" for Jim Hobson. I never had an orientation to The Company, and each time there was a question, several times a day, I had to call one of the District Managers. So I really never knew "who was who" at the company headquarters in St. Louis

Messrs:

Please review the Telephone Expense recap and your individual calls.

We wish to thank those of you who have concentrated effort on reducing total calls, total cost and average cost per call. As you can see, we have been able to reduce our overall phone expenses 14.90 1977 vs 1976 for the month of March.

Thank you. Keep up the good work.

because I did not have any formal training for the position, I would call the other District Managers almost daily to find out how to perform my duties. Bruno would send a letter out monthly with each field manager's phone charges. The manager with the highest amount would have his name circled in red. Guess who received this dubious distinction every month? This was typical of Bruno's Machiavellian management style.

TELEPHONE EXPENSE

PERIOD FROM: _____ 1977 TO: _____ 1977

SIGN	TOTAL CALLS	TOTAL COST	AVG. COST PER CALL	% '16 19%	TOTAL CALLS	TOTAL COST	AVG. COS PER CA..
	41	79.54					
	30	46.11	1.54		34	49.59	1.4
	29	53.74	1.85		71	100.31	1.4
	2	1.95	.98		6	11.25	1.74
	18	42.28	2.35		24	51.45	2.16
	120	223.62	1.86		158	247.61	1.5

	1977	%	1976	
COST PER CALL	1.86	+17.7	1.58	
COST PER MAN	44.72	-10.4	49.93	
CALL PER MAN	24	-25.6	32	

18.60 - Mind
627.92 - Cbw
STATEMENT TOTAL $ 646.52

$737.51

A few months after my promotion, Donald Miles was promoted to Region III, Black Markets Manager, a pre-retirement
position for him. Shortly thereafter, Rick Gates, Area Manager
for Michigan, was promoted to District Manager. Rick
relocated from Detroit to East Lansing, Michigan, home of
Michigan State University. I always envied Rick in that his
boss was Michael St. John, a younger, modern guy with a
master's degree. Michael's persona permeated throughout the
men in his division. It always seemed as though their mission
was gaining market share for The Company; they didn't seem
to participate in the covert activity that characterized the group
in Ohio. Once Rick relocated to Lansing, I would occasionally
make the four-hour drive there to get training on product
inventory management and writing the varied reports. Although
Rick, being Black, did not go through a formal training program for District Manager, the veteran District Managers in
Michigan had been eager to train him. So it was through these
kinds of tactics that I learned my job.

Company cars were leased through Fleet Enterprises
Leasing Company. There were minor charges for using the car
for personal driving. The problem with having only one car
was that you had to notify your Division Manager three weeks
in advance if you wanted to drive the car outside of the district.
So for me, if I wanted to drive to Detroit to purchase a tie or
pair of shoes or spend a day, I had to make that decision three
weeks in advance. With the constant changes in schedules, the
last minute assignments and the normal 68 hour minimum
work load, it was impossible to plan three weeks out. I was a
captive of Toledo, Ohio.

Oscar

A couple of months went by and there was not a word ever mentioned about the inquisition or the drive-by! Then one Monday in November, Lynn Thaxton, Bruno's secretary, called and asked if I planned to adhere to my itinerary, and if I would be in Toledo on Thursday (just out of curiosity!) I had "seen this, done that" before, or as the French would say, "deja vu."

On Tuesday, Lynn again called regarding a trivial matter, not worth the dime for the call, and then there was the "Oh by the way, will you be in Toledo on Thursday?" Does this sound familiar, are we starting to see a pattern? Once again I spoke with Titus Marlowe's attorney, Scott Vaughn, and Mr. Leimert. Both gentlemen agreed with my gut feelings, Bruno was up to something on Thursday.

Wednesday afternoon, Bruno called me at the Toledo Wholesaler Operation. After some trivial conversation, he informed me that Richard Stone, the Region Manager, wanted to meet me Thursday at 10 a.m. in the coffee shop of the Holiday Inn in South Bend, Indiana. Bruno asked me to come to the division office in Columbus, once I concluded my meeting with Richard. South Bend is midway between Toledo and Chicago, about a two-hour drive. After my conversation with Bruno, I tried to anticipate what this meeting could be about? Was it about Michael Goldberg, Titus Marlowe, Helen Barken, the molestation accusation, or was it something new? After all, I had been employed by The Company seventeen months. It was indeed about time for some new kind of crisis or clandestine activity. I was getting a rush of adrenaline in anticipation of Thursday.

Thursday morning I left Toledo extra early. I wanted to insure that I was in the coffee shop before Richard Stone. Richard was very late, he was very apologetic about his tardiness. Richard was in a jovial mood and told me what a great job I was doing, of how pleased Bruno was with my performance. Even Bill Teller, Vice President of Sales, was pleased.

Suddenly, Richard pulled a sheet of paper from his briefcase and began tearing it up! As he was tearing the paper to shreds, he stated that this was the only copy, and that his wife, Dolores, had typed it only last night at their kitchen table. Only four people knew of its existence: Bill Teller, Richard Stone, his wife and now me. Not even Bruno Pittman knew of its existence. Richard then handed me a sheet of paper, it was a letter of reprimand which did not include any names, dates, locations, but only that any such reoccurring incidents would be cause for termination. I simply replied, "bullshit." Richard agreed and stated that out of this adversity, I could rise like a shooting star in the company. Richard Stone, for his performance, should have been nominated for the Academy Award for his performance! We shook hands and I departed for Columbus.

During the four-hour drive to Columbus, I reviewed the events up to now. It was all so clear—what the attorneys and I suspected was now coming to fruition. My promotion to a district that was not conducive for a Black manager, and with this unofficial charge, was designed to pit me against Titus Marlowe. To give me a sense of frustration, insecurity, and wouldn't-I-do-anything-to-transfer-to-a-metropolitan/cosmopolitan city.

Wouldn't I agree that in lieu of all this, that Bruno and The Company had been very good to me.

It was late by the time I arrived at the division office, almost 5 p.m. Bruno was so congenial, he knew the emotional trauma I had just been through. It was then that he began to incriminate himself.

Bruno went on to say that on the day that I was moving to Toledo, Steve Lyons flew to Columbus regarding the Titus Marlowe case. While the two were having lunch, Steve presented Bruno the letter of reprimand that he had written to me and asked Bruno to sign. Bruno stated that "there was no evidence of my guilt and that he did not believe in The Company's tactics." Additionally, in light of the Titus Marlowe case, he was already viewed as a racist and this would not help his image. Besides, he and I were friends.

Accordingly, Steve told Bruno that not signing could adversely affect his career with The Company. Bruno went on to say that for some reason, he didn't know why, after lunch, he drove past my apartment, and he and Steve observed me on the porch the day I was moving. And so, on the day of the "drive-by," the Black man in Bruno's car had been Steve Lyons. I never revealed to Bruno that I observed them driving by or that Richard told me he had composed the letter and that his wife typed it and that not even Bruno knew of its existence. I was now learning the art of the game.

I was traveling so much and my lifestyle was such that about the only bills I had were rent and electricity for the refrigerator. I decided that under the circumstances, it did not make sense to try to adapt or make a home in Toledo. I would just continue to save my money until the final straw came.

Things were going along status quo when one day Bruno called to say that Richard Stone had been demoted from V.P. of Regional Sales to Branch Manager in Southern California. His replacement was Phillip Jones who was being transferred from Atlanta, Georgia. I didn't feel any sympathy for Richard, what goes around comes around, and after all, he was going to California.

Toni

8

I had decided to have my annual dental checkup and cleaning. As it so happened, the dentist's wife happened to be in the office that day. She and I exchanged the usual information like where I was from, yes I was not married, and no I did not know many people socially in the city. A few days later, she called and asked if I would like to have a home-cooked meal at their home that weekend.

Wow, home cooking. At dinner, I was told that there was an ulterior motive. They wanted to introduce me to a friend visiting from Los Angeles, California. I was leaving town for a two-week assignment in Memphis, Tennessee, so it was decided that my blind date and I would meet at a restaurant near the airport.

The restaurant was Oliver's, an upscale diner. We were to meet a couple of hours before my flight. With my bags packed and in the trunk of the car, I was at the restaurant on time to meet the blind date. I was drinking coffee waiting for the daughter of Frankenstein to come walking through the door.

I was thinking, "I paid good money for the dental services rendered," what more did I have to do, plus she was late. Much to my surprise and delight, this vision of loveliness walked up to me and asked if I was Jim. I couldn't believe my eyes, this goddess was sitting across the small table and in just a couple of minutes I had to leave for the airport.

I was taken away by how easy she was to talk to. Her obvious intelligence, style of dress, and cosmopolitan manner were very attractive. Her name was Toni. She was very apologetic about being late. I had to leave but asked if I could have her number so I could call from Memphis, she said, "Yes." I would have gotten down on my knees and begged her for the number, but I had a plane to catch. We walked out to the cars, I couldn't bear the thought that I would not be able to see her for two weeks. Life can be so unfair. I didn't know how or when, but I knew this was the girl I was going to marry.

In Memphis Tennessee, all I could think about was Toni. Breakfast, lunch and dinner I thought about her. I flew back to Toledo over the weekend and contacted my dentist's wife to get more information. Toni had gone to Cleveland for the weekend, her cousin was getting married soon there. I was, however, able to get her address.

When I arrived back in Memphis the first free moment I got, I mailgrammed a dozen yellow roses to her. The second week in Memphis went by as slow as the first. For the first time, I couldn't wait to get back to Toledo, Ohio.

Upon my return, I had my dentist's wife contact Toni regarding a date. She replied perhaps I could give her a call towards the end of the week. That meant a long week in gray, desolate Toledo. Finally, Friday came and wow, she accepted a dinner invitation for Saturday. If I had been in a city where you could buy clothes off the rack, I would have purchased an outfit just for the occasion.

At dinner, I was able to find out that she had a bachelor's and master's degree from two top California universities. She was an only child and was on an extended visit to Toledo. She was staying with her aunt and uncle, a prominent family in Toledo. I took her home and asked if I could see her again, she said, "Perhaps." That evening I looked at my apartment and thought, this will never do, this beautiful lady was going to take a lot to be impressed.

On Sunday, I went to the shopping center and ordered a couch, cocktail table, lamps, etc., all from the catalog. I told the sales people I would call back on Monday with an address to deliver the furniture. On Monday, during lunch, I rented an aesthetically pleasing two-bedroom apartment. (Love is crazy, love makes you do foolish things.) I signed a one-year lease.

During the week I would be in other cities, but now Toni was amendable to dinner or a movie on weekends. If she ever wondered why I never invited her to my apartment, it was because I was waiting to move. There was no time for me to try to sell my humble furniture, so I donated it to charity.

One month later, I moved into my new apartment with virtually only boxes. A few days later, my furniture arrived. Now, I was ready for entertaining. I had smoked cigarettes since my senior year in high school until the time I met Toni. She was the incentive I needed to quit.

I was smoking a pack a day, and always wanted to quit. When I was in college, I thought I'd quit just as soon as I got out of college, when the pressure of midterms and finals were over. Then I went into the military and I said as soon as I get out of the military and the pressures of military life were over I would quit smoking. Then, it was the pressure of my first real employment with real responsibility. I always found a new stress in my life to replace an old one, and that kept me smoking.

But meeting Toni, somehow, was the motivation I needed to quit smoking, and I think if not that day, then one of the next few days while I was in Memphis I threw the pack of cigarettes away for good! I still hated the city, the district, working for Bruno, but now Phillip Jones proved to be a welcomed distraction for Bruno. Phillip Jones was a no-nonsense manager who apparently did not play the "good ole boy" game, at least not with the Midwestern Region field personnel. He wanted sales, "not excuses and scapegoats."

Toni and I were getting pretty close, but by now I was feeling pretty insecure. The economy in the mid-west was terrible. Every year the Midwestern Region field managers would retreat to a resort. It was designed to be some work, some play, each District Manager had to give a presentation on the state of his district. Sales were bad for The Company throughout the mid-west. The automotive industry was in desperate straits, maybe a precursor of things to come.

I started my presentation with "Michigan sneezed and Ohio caught the cold." It was a long held sentiment that the brewing industry was virtually recession-proof, but people in the depressed areas were purchasing popular priced beers. It seemed only a crazy person would purchase a house in a city with such a depressed housing market.

Toni and her family introduced me to several people who had found jobs in the sunbelt, but they could not sell their homes even at a fraction of the market value. Up to now I had never told Toni how precarious my own position was with The Company. She could see how conscientious and professional I was. I would check into hotels during the winter and look out the windows in the evenings at the desolate areas in Marion, Lorain, Bellevue and think I could not bear much more. I was in a real dilemma about what to do about Toni.

The Corporate Lynching 9

It was during one of the coldest weeks of that winter that Bruno called a meeting in Columbus. One of my wholesalers in Marion was just off the highway en route to Columbus. I took advantage of being in such close proximity to Marion to stop and conduct some business.

It was past noon by the time I arrived at the Division office; everyone except for Lynn, Bruno's secretary had left for lunch. It was very cold, and it was snowing, I was just going to forego lunch, but Lynn stated that Bruno was insistent that I join them.

I joined the group at Michael's, a restaurant we often frequented. I had no problem locating them, they were seated at a large, round table—Bruno, the District Managers Robert Gladstone, Tom Johnson, Louie Scott (who had been promoted) and two gentlemen I had never seen before. As I was shaking everyone's hand, Bruno expressed his concern for my well-being driving in the inclement weather. He proceeded to introduce me to the strangers by name only.

During lunch it was never mentioned who these gentlemen were. In fact, as we departed the restaurant, I told the gentlemen that it was nice to have made their acquaintance. Needless to say, I was surprised when the strangers met us back at the office. As I was taking off my coat, Bruno asked me to step into his office. In his office were the strangers again. Bruno revealed that they were attorneys from Sutton, Bacon, and Fox and they wanted to talk to me.

Deja vu! This was it! All of their planning, underhandedness, my promotion to a rural district, the molestation charge, the reprimand that did not exist, the non-existent meeting with Richard Stone in South Bend, Indiana, all came down to this. I was caught off guard. There was no preemptive questioning where I would be today. I sat in Bruno's chair. They sat in the two chairs in front of Bruno's desk. I assumed that the attorneys and Bruno figured that the element of surprise coupled with the two of them bombarding me with questions, would intimidate me to say and/or agree with anything.

As in the case of my meeting with Richard Stone in South Bend, the meeting started out well. They went on about how Bruno admired my performance and admired me as a person. Then their tone began to change and the questions came faster.

They asked if I was aware of Titus Marlowe's discrimination case against Bruno and The Company. Had I ever met or had conversation with Marlowe and/or Scott Vaughn? Of course. I had to inquire as to who Scott Vaughn was, to which they replied, he was of no consequence. Wouldn't I agree that Bruno and The Company had been "very good to me?" And, after all, didn't Bruno stand by me in my moment of peril with the molestation charge?

Finally, they asked if I were called to court on Bruno's behalf, how would I testify, would I in fact testify that during my employment Bruno and The Company had treated me more than fairly?

It all came down to this, my trials and tribulations, hopes and aspirations, my future, my career came down to this moment. A "yes" and perhaps The Company Wholesalership or, at the very least, a promotion to a "cushy" over-paid job in California or Hawaii. A "no" and the catalyst to my corporate demise, or even worse, the rest of my life in Toledo, Ohio. The straw that breaks the camel's back or the straw that stirs the drink. Which would it be?

Was I standing for something, could I turn my back on my brother? After all, it didn't seem to bother Steve Lyons. There was no question that Bruno was a racist, that Titus Marlowe's and Leo Sampson' demises were fostered, if not precipitated, by the "good ole boy" network.

And what of my own situation? This time I could not take a neutral position as I had with Helen. Now, I was being called to act. What would be my reward, if any? There is a saying at The Company: "Management only remembers what you did for them today."

And what next—what would I be asked to do tomorrow? How would the Blacks in the company view me, as a turncoat, an Uncle Tom? Would I be alienated or shunned by them? What if the general public found out I testified against two Blacks that were obviously railroaded?

What about all of the Blacks that were killed in the fifties and sixties, and jailed in the seventies? What was my allegiance to the civil rights marches I saw on television as a child, the conversations my elders had about racism and discrimination in the work place? Would I now be looked upon as the "House Nigger" that told of the slaves' plans to escape? The divide and conquer sentiment obviously prevailed when it came to Blacks. Steve Lyons against Jim Hobson, Jim Hobson against Titus Marlowe and Leo Sampson, who knows what other Black scenarios were being played out across the country?

There was a long pause, it was as if my so-called career flashed before my eyes. I took a deep breath, AND I SAID NO!

The attorneys were flabbergasted, they had been so sure of themselves, these high-priced legal eagles. All of Bruno's and The Company's manipulation, the time they must have put into their poorly executed devious plans. Where had they gone wrong? How could they have misjudged my response? Had all of their underhandedness driven me from being hard-working and blindly dedicated to now independent of their manipulation? Had they pushed once too much, dangled the carrot for far too long? The attorneys asked if I would reconsider my answer. I said no!

They immediately jumped from their chairs and told me I could leave. As I exited the office, they signaled Bruno to come in. The three were in the office a short time. A few moments later, the attorneys left, they didn't even say good-bye. An hour or so later, the District Managers left to go home. Bruno's only words after the attorneys left were have a safe trip.

During the drive back to Toledo, I thought about what had transpired that afternoon, and on the many days and nights during my employment. I knew it was over, and perhaps just as well, it was time for my agony to end. There was only one formality left, telling Toni I would soon be jobless.

Returning to Toledo, I contemplated selling the furniture I had so recently purchased. I started searching the used car lots for the car I would soon need.

About a week went by before Bruno called. He was joyous and jubilant. I had never heard his voice so happy. The Company knew that they had a losing proposition, so they stretched it out as long as they could (from 1977 to 1981) hoping Titus Marlowe would run out of steam or money. At the final moment, well, lets' just say it came to a conclusion.

Finally, my long ordeal was over, my perseverance had paid off, the dark cloud over Columbus, Ohio had now vanished. No reason now for covert activities, now I could focus on the positives—my career, Toni, the great American Dream.

For a few weeks, things actually seemed to be better, but they got worse just as fast. With the Marlowe case no longer hanging over his head, Bruno's true identify surfaced, his ubiquitous ego became energized. It was as if he was given carte blanche to say and do anything to anybody, any time he pleased.

During this same time, the Warren, Ohio wholesalers, and the Volante Family, were attempting to purchase the Cleveland, Ohio wholesale operation. Bruno did not like this at all. Also, I noticed that his relationship with Tom Johnson, the District Manager for Cleveland, was starting to deteriorate.

However, it was life as usual on our visits to Columbus. We would still go out and drink and drink and drink night after night. Only now, Tom Johnson was no longer part of the clique. During those evening sessions, Bruno would talk about Tom in such a derogatory manner. I had a sense that the problem started a long time ago, but was being manifested by the Volante Family's proposed purchase of the Cleveland wholesalership.

Alan Volante was a personal friend of Bill Teller, V. P. of Sales. In spite of the close proximity of Warren to Cleveland, Bruno felt that Alan should live in Cleveland. To appease Bruno, Alan rented an apartment in Cleveland pending the sale.

One day, in what had become a rarity, Tom Johnson joined the group for lunch. You could have cut the tension between him and Bruno with a knife. As we were leaving the restaurant, I remarked about a new pair of glasses Tom was wearing. Bruno remarked that I should knock the glasses off of Tom's face.

The Cleveland Ohio Wholesale Operation.

Tom would seldom join the group for lunch when we were in Columbus, and never joined the group on the drinking campaigns. During the evenings, Bruno would talk about Tom in a derogatory manner. Now Lynn Thaxton, who had been Bruno's conduit in many of the covert activities, was the brunt of his jokes and criticism. Bruno had no fears of reprisals from The Company for the mean treatment to his subordinates. What scheme would Bruno devise to get rid of Lynn, a single mother, and what role would I be asked to play?

One day while I was working at the wholesalers operation in Lorain, Lynn called, there was so much emotion in her voice. Lynn wanted to talk, in particular I remember our conversation regarding Louis Scott. Earlier in the book, I commented on how Louis would leave Columbus to spend the weekends with his fiancée at Ball State in Muncie, Indiana. For whatever reason, and I guess only God knows why, Bruno did not like this.

So, on many Friday afternoons, Lynn would locate Louie and give him an assignment to be completed immediately. The irony was that she withheld the assignments until Fridays, and in most cases accelerated the due dates long before it was really due.

Again, deja vu! How many times had this same scenario been played out, with Titus Marlowe, Leo Sampson, Helen Barken, Jim Hobson, and now young Louie?

Poor Lynn, a single parent, was coerced into hurting people she worked with and actually liked. It was Lynn who befriended Helen Barken, they met at the ballet school their daughters attended. It was Lynn who convinced Helen to apply for the position with The Company.

Now Lynn bore the brunt of Bruno's wrath, and I guess she knew that soon she, too, would be victimized. Lynn, in an attempt to develop a better life for herself and her daughter, took on the rigors of night school and was awarded a bachelor's degree. Now the entire Ohio contingent had at least bachelor's degrees, all except for Bruno. The strain that was etched on my face from the "intentional infliction of emotional distress" was now to become etched on my co-workers' faces. Additionally, Lynn was forced to track Tom, to call his wholesalers to see if he was there or how long it took him to get to different locations.

Targeting the Black market, The Company in particular has developed programs in large Black communities to which they donate money, which is not even a fraction of the profits they make from Blacks. They have a dozen or so Blacks that they have pinned these mega-titles on, whose sole job is to attend all the annual Black conventions, e.g., NAACP, Urban League, Black Nurses' Association, Black Dentist Convention, Congressional Black Caucus, etc., and give a party. At these public relations parties, Black V.P.'s will donate a few thousand dollars on behalf of "Bratbrau" to this worthy group. It is unfortunate, indeed, that the two highest ranking Blacks were "Vice Presidents of Public Relations."

Those corporate Black employees with those impressive titles, such as Regional Manager, have no one at all reporting to them. They are relegated to sponsoring the local golf, tennis and bid whist tournaments. They are cardboard managers with no clout, doomed to a life of isolation and meaninglessness. But, they pop up at Black functions with smiling faces and handshakes, at the whim of corporate management. Just to keep Black people smiling and drunk, and themselves fat with all of their profits.

All of this effort to make the upper echelon Blacks feel important, so that their less fortunate brethren will drink more Bratbrau, so they, too, can ascend to being important. I guess I think I feel this way because I have been inside the corporate ranks and I have been victimized. I hate to open a Black magazine or newspaper and see how nice The Company has been to niggers! I guess if white folks could buy the island of Manhattan from the Indians for some beads and blankets, their descendants can buy Black loyalty to Bratbrau for a "party."

Historically, Blacks have been victimized by alcohol. The negative effects of alcohol during emancipation have been well-documented. Alcohol has been the root cause of Black family dissolution for years, and in most cases, the first step toward drug abuse. Over the past decade, there has been an awakening by white America that its youth were displaying the ill effects of alcohol and drugs. Such groups as MADD: Mothers Against Drunk Drivers, have surfaced to curtail or regulate alcohol advertising and promotion.

In response to the negative publicity and the public's perception of the beer industry, The Company developed programs dealing with the issue of alcohol abuse. In reality, how many of these programs have filtered down to Blacks? With the "Browning of America" and with minorities' birth rates higher than the national average, and the per capita consumption of alcohol declining in white America, more and more programs are being targeted at minorities. It would be a good college project to measure the correlation between targeting alcohol to minorities and the rates of minority crime, incarceration, and drug use.

A Prominent Civil Rights Leader: My Reprieve

10

In September 1981, things were terrible. Bruno's wrath knew no bounds, sales were down and morale among the Ohio Field Marketing personnel and the wholesalers was very low. I was in love with Toni, but knew my position was precarious, it was a day-to-day call as to what to expect from Bruno. The Columbus, Ohio wholesaler decided to distribute Canadian Import Beer. This angered Bruno to no end.

In retaliation, Bruno summoned Robert Gladstone, Tom Johnson and myself, along with Louie Scott and Victor Turner, to crew the market. "Crew" meant work the market and look for problems on the wholesaler. All of us felt bad about this activity. The Livingstons were a great family, they had always gone out of their way to be nice and cooperative, they had one of the premiere The Company Wholesalerships in the country.

During that week, there was little camaraderie among us. A sense of evil and ugliness prevailed. There was no longer a feeling of being a team. Even the wholesaler personnel no longer smiled.

Finally Friday arrived, we assembled in the Columbus Wholesaler's conference room, along with the Livingstons and their management, to critique the week's findings. In an unprecedented act and a page out of Jim Hobson's book of James Bond 007, Bruno placed his Lanier recorder on the conference table. Bruno opened the meeting by stating who was in attendance, then he proceeded to ask each The Company field manager what he found or observed in the marketplace. Each of us in turn stated that we had no negative findings or observations in the marketplace. Bruno had fired a blank once again.

The following Wednesday evening, Bruno called me at home with some startling but welcomed news. Bruno had been summoned to St. Louis and met with the Vice President of Sales, Bill Teller. Bruno was dismissed as Division Manager of Ohio. He was ordered to clear his personal items from the office, and to wait at home until such time as a determination was made about his future. I, of course, wished him the best of luck, and as I laid the telephone receiver down, I let out the loudest yell and jumped for joy. Coincidentally, the very same week, Tom Johnson, the Cleveland District Manager that had disputes with Bruno, was promoted to Military Sales Manager!

The news about Bruno called for a celebration. I asked Toni to marry me, and she said yes. I was assigned to cover Tom Johnson's wholesalers. I was covering all of Northern Ohio, I was really busy and loving every minute of it. I had to steal time on the weekends to see Toni. I guess that there is some truth to the cliché, "absence makes the heart grow fonder." Months went by before a new Division Manager was appointed. Ohio was in such a state that several Managers in the corporation refused the Division Manager's position. Finally, Mike Peterson was assigned. The Ohio managers were elated, Mike had been manager of the "Management Development" department for The Company.

Mike was a breath of fresh air compared to Bruno. He grew up in the Detroit area and graduated from the University of Detroit. He played pro football with a major NFL team, was a trainer with the Detroit Pistons, taught English and coached high school football. Prior to joining The Company, he had been a high ranking manager with a mid-western Brewing Company. Mike's lifelong experiences, including sports and the military, helped developed his character and rapport with minorities.

People skills were his strong trait. He could work with all types of people and he was a motivator! Mike's first order of business was to move the office to a more modern, larger office building on the top floor.

Out with the old furniture and in with the new. The offices were decorated in crimson and gray, the Ohio State University colors. Then there was the week at "Old Saw Mill Creek" resort in Sandusky, Ohio. It was a week of rest and relaxation, morning meetings, and then golf, fishing, tennis, racquetball, whatever. This was a team and there was morale building to be done, the breaking down of the defensiveness each of us had from the previous tyranny. In the meetings, we brainstormed and budgeted for the next year, and it appeared as if we could finally focus on the competition and marketing of The Company products.

The next step was raising the morale of the Ohio wholesalers and their personnel. Titus Marlowe had been reprimanded by Bruno for spending too much money on post-conventions. These were yearly functions that wholesalers literally had to beat their sales personnel to attend. These dull meetings were held in drab hotels in each District Manager's headquarter's city.

Mike decided that there would be two post-conventions instead of four—Cleveland for northern Ohio and Cincinnati for southern Ohio. Instead of a weeknight, we would make it a weekend gala event. The entire wholesaler personnel were invited along with their significant other.

During the meetings, Mike announced that a Chevrolet Corvette would be awarded to the top Driver/Salesman at the end of the year. Also during the meeting, Mike would break to raffle a prize to the audience. The meeting was conducted while everyone sat down to a first class dinner.

After dinner, there was a gala dance, and it was a most enjoyable evening for everyone. The Company picked up the tab for the hotel rooms. The only out of pocket expense for the wholesaler was transportation. We were turning the corner with regard to morale, people were starting to smile again!

Marriage

It was in this comfortable atmosphere that Toni and I were married. We honeymooned in the Bahamas and for a while I was on top of the world. Finally, this kid from Chicago's ghetto had it all, everything that was supposed to come from education, hard work and most of all sacrifice.

Life was not all rosy, of course. Toni was unable to find a job in her chosen field, so she went to work for her aunt and uncle in the mortuary business as an apprentice Funeral Director. And there were the weeks I would be on the road. Toledo was now proving to be not only a city I disliked, but one Toni disliked as well.

She was having difficulty adjusting to a small mid-western blue-collar town. I was being torn again; now I had a job that I liked, but we were stuck in an unsuitable city.

Boycott

A Mid-Western Civil Rights Organization had as its President a prominent civil rights leader from the sixties. The Organization had singled out The Company for refusing to be fair to Blacks, although taking huge profits from the Black community. The Organization accused The Company of not hiring, promoting, or doing business with enough minority members. The Organization's Leader met with the President of The Company and their differences could not be reconciled. A boycott of The Company and its brand, particularly Bratbrau, was initiated. The boycott was endorsed by prominent civil rights leaders in Atlanta, Georgia. Additionally, several Black Mayors of major cities, and city council members, also endorsed the boycott. This was a serious boycott, it was featured in the *Wall Street Journal* on February 1, 1983 issue on page 27.

The Organization's Leader would fly to cities across the country holding news conferences regarding the boycott. As the news media watched, The Organization's Leader would pop the top of a can of Bratbrau and pour it to the ground. The Organization contended that of the 950 wholesalers of The

Company, there was only one Black, and there were not many Blacks in viable management positions.

Now my paranoia was about to go into overdrive, again the reality of my plight was hanging in the balance. My father and namesake, James M. Hobson, Sr. in his sixties, retired, and having seen his children enter their chosen professions, now turned that determination and dedication to The Organization. My namesake could not play any role, but only a highly visible and most assuredly dangerous one, but one he could fulfill with passion—that of bodyguard and security chief to The Organization's President and his family.

As a result of the boycott, The Organization's President and his family received numerous death threats! Federal government police agencies and the local city police were holding periodic briefings regarding possible assassination attempts, the threats were very real! A picture of The Organization's President with a red bulls eye painted about the face was being circulated around the country. Dr. Martin Luther King's assassination and the mystery and/or conspiracy surrounding it still haunted Black America. By now my father's dedication to The Organization and its president was well known in and around the Organization. Any individual or group targeting The Organization's President or family would first or simultaneously have to murder my father. My sister and brothers were very worried, my mother, though worried, had resigned herself, my father was doing what he wanted to do, and she put her trust in God.

I knew my father would be no match against any conspiracy. The tormented inner feelings I had regarding Titus Marlowe, Leo Sampson, Helen Barken, the Jewish wholesalers, and others now somehow almost mythically engulfed my family.

I suspected The Company had spies in The Organization, I was sure they knew who my father was, and I figured I was being watched pretty closely. The atmosphere for Blacks in the shadow of the boycott was not too comfortable, and it was sometimes pretty hard to swallow the inflammatory remarks insinuated by my white male counterparts! On my many flights to The Company headquarters, I wondered if I would be confronted with exposure or become part of a plan that was devised through manipulation to achieve some devious solution to the boycott!

During a meeting in Chicago, while on a break, one of the Region Administrators congratulated me on winning the "Accent on Excellence Award." This award is given to the top District Manager in the country based on performance criteria that are evaluated by senior management. I had received what up to now had been "a prestigious award" without being evaluated. When I got back to the meeting, I asked Mike about the lack of evaluation for the award, he replied, "That's right," as he fixed his eyes on an object away from me. There were no congratulations. Mike was ashamed. Sean, who replaced Tom as District Manager for Cleveland, was quick to point out that I had only won the award because of the boycott.

A few weeks later, Toni and I flew first class to St. Louis to a dinner honoring me. Douglas O'Donald, a very perceptive Vice President of Marketing, made lots of nice comments and jokes. There were executive pictures and prizes. The prizes amounted to approximately $2,OOO. I never really knew the pay structure at The Company or the mechanics of how it all worked. The raise I received on my promotion to District

Manager was negligible, and I often wondered what my colleagues were earning.

On my next annual salary review (there was no actual interface) I received a 15% salary increase. Thank you, Civil Rights Leader! I felt that The Company thought that the Organization's President might find out the disparity in Black managers' salaries. Perhaps also senior management knew of all the racism I had been subjected to and they were attempting to appease me. I've often wondered if they thought I would join the Organization's ranks.

I had worked hard for The Company, through many sacrifices, trials and tribulations. I was deserving of the salary increases and awards. I had seen many District Managers promoted who I thought were less deserving. Now, during the boycott, I became promotable. I literally depleted the Division's annual budget flying to St. Louis for interviews. I would get calls on just about a weekly basis from Mike or a manager in St. Louis to fly out there. First, I interviewed with Brian Bennett, Vice President of Brand Management. The following week I interviewed with the Leafbrau Brand Manager. Then I was back to interview for Target States Manager, then back for Dimension of Excellence coordinator, and back again for Pricing Coordinator.

Then there was a day of marathon interviews with members of the various brand teams: Bratbrau, Brat Light, Leafbrau Light and Clarity.

Under other circumstances, it would have been gratifying to interview for such positions, but in the shadow of the boycott I felt manipulated, this was all just another facade. Once again, the company was attempting to position me against another Black. I felt I would be just a token Black being used as window dressing.

Besides The Company's employment practices, the Civil Rights Leader pointed out that of the 950 Company wholesalers, only one or 0.1% was Black. My Findlay, Ohio wholesaler, Edward Calderon, was also President of the Ohio Wholesale Beer Association. During their annual convention in Cleveland, Edward had dinner with Hirsh H. Heidenthal. Hirsh informed Edward that several of The Company-owned wholesalerships in urban markets had been selected for sale to Blacks.

Armed with that information, Edward lost no time in asking me to come to Findlay the following week. Over lunch, Edward proposed that we jointly acquire The Company Wholesalership in an urban market, and he would finance the acquisition.

Finally, after kicking myself for years for moving to Toledo, the years of lies and manipulation, now just maybe, maybe it was all going to payoff. Maybe it was worth it after all. The Company owned wholesalerships throughout the country. Toni was excited at the prospect of moving to a metropolitan, if not cosmopolitan city, as well as perhaps finding a job in her chosen profession.

I was one of three Black District Managers. I thought this, coupled with financing from my wholesaler, would give me a competitive edge for the acquisition. However, if push came to shove, I was prepared to play hardball. I decided to contact the NCRF in Columbus for insurance. It was a great reunion, everyone familiar with the Bruno Pittman scenario was excited about the prospect of me becoming a wholesaler.

I met with several business attorneys who were counseled on what had transpired the previous years. The attorneys wanted to discuss my situation, and explore the different avenues, and so I left with a promise that they would get back to me. In the meantime, Edward Calderon wrote Hirsh Heidenthal a letter regarding the wholesale acquisition. Edward pointed out how a Black had been his District Manager for several years, and how impressed he was with my dedication and professionalism. Edward wrote of his capability of financing such an operation and my willingness to relocate to another city. A few weeks passed before there was any response. First, there was the letter from the attorneys.

I felt good about the letter, now I had a white legal firm telling me that indeed the acts were racism. A few days later, Edward received a letter from Hirsh. It simply stated that our request had been turned over to Steve Lyons.

What a shock! I knew that Steve would be my nemesis, he would keep me from getting The Company wholesale operation!

27 October 1983

James Hobson
1805 Brownstone Boulevard
Toledo, Ohio 43614

Dear Mr. Hobson:

I have given considerable thought to the situation
you described to me during our conversation on October 20,
1983. I have discussed the same with several colleques
and the general consensus is the same.

While the situation is a fascinating one, I don't
believe your interests could be effectively advanced
through litigation. As I explained during our conversation,
many of the other matters you raised could have been the
subject of charges of race discrimination, however, such
charges must be filed within six months of the date of the
alleged violation. All the incidents you described could
not now be the subject of timely filed charges.

Finally, as to the distributorship I suggest you solicit
a status report from the company as regards your application.
If it is ultimately denied you should attempt to obtain the
company's reason therefor. At that point perhaps another
evaluation should be made.

Thank you for the opportunity to consider this matter
and do not hesitate to contact me if you have any questions.

Very Truly Yours,

I was married now and felt I could not be radical, and I still wanted to work through the system. If patience is a virtue, then I was the most virtuous person in the world. Days turned into weeks and weeks into months. I was holding out hope that miraculously I would get a call from Edward or St. Louis. It was agony, literally sitting on the documentation and tapes and wondering if I shouldn't just turn everything over to The Civil Rights Organization. After a few months, Hirsh had unofficially conceded to The Civil Rights Organization. Four Blacks were given partial ownership of three of The Company owned wholesale operations.

Colin Daley, who worked in St. Louis, was given minority ownership in the mid-west. The Black District Manager in the southeast, Daniel Spear, was given partial ownership there. Lastly, Jack Novak and Kenneth Clark, both Blacks, were given co-ownership in a western city.

And so I had missed my golden opportunity, I was buried in Toledo. Toni and I lived in an apartment, we both wanted a home but I was afraid that with the poor economy in Toledo, that if the opportunity ever came to leave, I would not be able to find a buyer. People were always asking when we were going to start a family. My work situation was so tenuous. I wanted to wait until we were located someplace else.

Very few companies, if any at all, come to Toledo to recruit for employment. On Sundays, I would go downtown and pay $4.50 for the *Los Angeles Times*. Most companies would only relocate in the region, and there was not much available in the mid-west. Additionally, it was virtually impossible to get away to other cities for interviews. I thought about just quitting The Company and going to a sunbelt city, leaving Toni behind until I found something. At the time, there were a couple of good reasons why that wouldn't work. First, Toni's job did not have medical benefits, second with one car, I would have to rent a car and stay in a hotel until I could find a job in a strange city.

When one thing in your life is not right, it can adversely affect everything else in your life. It's like the domino effect. I was trapped, I wonder now if I didn't somehow unconsciously blame Toni, as if she was the chain holding me to Toledo.

In retrospect, I wonder if Mike Peterson or the wholesalers noticed my loss of enthusiasm for the job. Certainly, I felt betrayed by The Company, my ego was crushed, I lost my self-confidence. I was out of my element, my comfort zone. I was a fish out of water. I had no identity, a young Black educated urbanite doing business in rural America.

Somewhere I read once that the white man could not enslave the Indians because they could not adjust to confinement and would simply die. I felt like that untamed Indian. Maybe it was my Indian blood, but my conservative image just didn't fit. My suits, ties, and business shoes were anachronistic in rural areas.

Sean pursued my friendship. For me he was a resource that I thought I needed since I hadn't gone through a training program at The Company. He was happily married and so was I. Both of us had matured past the bar scene, and so, on the many evenings in Columbus or other cities, we would pal up and do other things. We would try eating at different restaurants, go to the movies, and if there was a gym, we would go work out or play racquetball.

The hotel rooms were all starting to look alike. I would feel like a prisoner on those evenings when I was stuck in the room. Going out with Sean was a welcome distraction from the four walls of the hotel room. We would have a couple of drinks usually, but hardly more than that. Ironically, I would almost never drink except on those occasions when I was with my co-workers. I thought just hanging with Sean was a safe altern-ative. It was either that or hanging myself in my hotel room.

The Company held its convention in St. Louis in November 1984. I had just completed my sixth market report which for me was a ritual that kept me confined for weeks. Towards the end of a day of meetings and events, Sean asked if I wanted to go out for dinner which was okay by me. Later that evening, Sean called. It had been a long day and I had decided to just stay in and order room service. Sean tried to promote feelings of guilt in me, and responded, "Thanks a lot." He had showered and changed to go out to dinner.

After a bit of coaxing, I conceded to meeting him in the lobby. When I got to the lobby, there was Sean and much to my surprise, Dave and Paul, our advertising representatives from Davenport, Elliot, and Martin in Chicago. I had met Dave and Paul in Columbus on a couple of occasions. Dave had worked closely with Sean on a major promotion in Cleveland the previous year. I guess Sean and Dave had become friends. I remember thinking when I first saw them, if I had known Sean had someone to go dine with, I would have declined. I felt like saying that, but it would have been awkward, so I went along.

Sean and I were staying at the Stouffers Hotel, Dave and Paul at the Brittney about four blocks away in the heart of downtown St. Louis. We took a cab to The Gas Light, a renovated area of restaurants, bars and shops by the Mississippi River. We went to an Italian restaurant and had a truly magnificent dinner—salad, bread, pasta, dessert and of course, plenty of wine and Bratbrau. We laughed and joked together. It was a lighthearted evening, at least up to then.

When we left the restaurant, I thought it was best to find a taxi for the short trip back to our respective hotels, after all, it was around 10:30 or so and Sean and I had to be at the brewery in the morning.

The Bust

11

I was "high" from drinking so much, but I was not drunk, yet still not sober enough to drive a car. We left the restaurant and walked across the street. I thought to catch a taxi, but to my surprise, we walked into a bar. We were seated at a table and had a few more drinks, where I crossed the fine line between being "high" to being intoxicated.

I remember a white girl dancing on the dance floor, who kept pulling up her blouse and exposing her breasts (she was not wearing a bra.). Dave danced with her a couple of times and then brought her over to our table and introduced her. We then had a few more rounds of drinks. Finally, we left.

Unknown to me, Dave had propositioned the girl, which involved a drive back to the Brittney in downtown St. Louis. I must have been drunk to get into a car with someone who was drunker and perhaps crazier than I was. She parked across the street from the Brittney; I had hoped she would drop Sean and me off at the Stouffers, but I didn't mind walking, and the November night air would have done us good.

Sean was insistent on going to Dave's room, and I was reluctant to walk four blocks to the Stouffers on the desolate and dark streets alone. Through all of this, I had little conversation with Dave or Paul. I really didn't know these guys, and I was just sort of the odd man out. All of us went up to Dave's room. Later the girl went to the front desk in the lobby and stated she'd been raped. The police were called and the manager led them to Dave's room. Four policemen entered the room and ordered Dave, Sean and me to face the wall. Paul had left to go to his room upstairs. We were told we were being arrested for rape. I blurted, "You've got to be kidding!" Dave was more belligerent, he told them she was a lying whore. I was in a state of shock, more surprised, more in a state of disbelief than scared. Sean and I were escorted to the police van; it was embarrassing walking through the hotel lobby handcuffed. Thankfully, it was very late, and not many people were in the lobby. Dave stayed in his room while two of the officers searched it.

It was Sean and I and the two police officers in a large room with typewriters and desks, very much like the one depicted in the Barney Miller television series. The handcuffs were removed and the police took our names, home addresses, etc. The atmosphere was pretty relaxed, Sean and I walked around free to go to the bathrooms, drink coffee and have general conversation with the police. The police were very congenial, they had been around, they knew the girl had not been raped.

Even at this point, my main concern was getting back to the hotel, showering, getting to the brewery on time, and getting through the day with no sleep.

A couple of hours later, the other police brought Dave in. Dave had stayed behind to be present while his room was searched. Then he went to the hospital with the girl, she was examined to see if in fact sexual activity had occurred. There were certainly no physical signs of force, such as bruises, scratches or fractures.

I knew then it was going to be a long night because the police now wanted to know who the fourth guy was. Paul had left to go to his room and was unaware of what was going on. The three of us were handcuffed together and were escorted through a door. Now, the nightmare was truly about to begin.

We were led to a room with two very large, dimly lit cells. We were escorted to a small barred window and ordered to place all of our valuables in a box, then we were led into the cell with about forty other inmates. We were now occupants with the worst elements St. Louis had to offer, the dregs of society. Dressed in my camel hair sports coat and button down white shirt, I felt particularly vulnerable in this setting with two ivy league white boys. It was also particularly distressing coming into this kind of environment in a strange city early in the morning. I could see the nervousness in Sean's and Dave's faces, I put my arms around them and told them to hang tough. I think I was more just trying to psych myself.

Sean pulled out his cigarettes and in a matter of seconds the prison vultures begged the pack away. Of course, Sean didn't refuse.

About 30 feet away were a few women in a large cell. The men and women were yelling back and forth about sexual conduct, I guess it was a way of passing the time. My mind now had turned to survival, I was now around the element I grew up with, a fight was imminent. I was trying to inch Sean and Dave to one of the walls in the cell. I figured we would have a better chance fighting in front with our backs to the wall, rather than going down in the middle of the pack. About 45 minutes passed, I didn't have my watch, when I heard the prison bus pull into the garage. The door to the garage opened and several police walked in dragging a long, heavy chain with handcuffs attached. People started stirring, I thought we were about to be transferred to a county jail.

A policeman opened the cell door and called out Dave's, Sean's and my names. The three of us piled out of the cell and much to my surprise, were led to an elevator, where we were taken upstairs to a floor lined with cells. We entered a vacant cell, it had dark gray metal walls. At the rear was a metal toilet with no seat, across the walkway was a barred window that had been coated with something so that you could not see out.

After a few hours had passed, the jailer opened the cell door and we were led back to the elevator. Without a word from the jailer, we were led to the barred window next to the holding cell, the holding cell now was only partially filled from the morning roundup by police. We signed for our personal belongings, I couldn't believe we were being released. We were led through a number of locked doors before we were met by our attorney's assistant in the lobby of the building. The attorney drove us to our respective hotels, en route he told us that once we cleaned up, and straightened out the matter with our employers, we should come to his office that afternoon. The message light was flashing when I entered my hotel room, I called the front desk immediately. The message was to meet Vince Kelly, an assistant to Dan Dezenso, V.P. of Sales in the lobby of the St. Louis Convention Center in a couple of hours. I ordered room service, I showered, the hot water was great, I almost washed my troubles away. Room service came and my meal was also great. I was now ready to interface with the powers that be at The Company.

Sean and I met in the hotel's lobby and took a taxi to the St. Louis Convention Center. Vince Kelly gave us each envelopes, the letter from Dan Dezenso, V.P. of Sales, simply stated that we were not to conduct business on behalf of The Company until further notice. We called Dave and told him to meet us at the attorney's office in a St. Louis suburb. The attorney informed us that we were being freed pending a decision from the District Attorney on what to do regarding our case. We took a taxi to the Airport, en route we talked about our situation and our wives.

Sean and Dave were going to tell their wives immediately, I couldn't. Sean offered to call Toni to try to explain how this could have happened. I said perhaps later. We shook hands at the Airport terminal, wished each other luck and proceeded to our respective gates. On the plane, I thought about Toni, what I would tell her if anything, and what about our future, if any. That evening, I acted as if everything was o.k. I told Toni that I had a nice time in St. Louis, but was glad to be home.

The Charade

The next morning I told Toni that I was going to work in my home office. After she left for work, I called Mike Peterson at the Division Office. Much to my chagrin Mike was on the line with Sean, so I had to talk with Lynn. I was told that while we were jailed, a police official called Hirsh H. Heidenthal and told him of our plight. Consequently, that morning Hirsh called a meeting with all of the field marketing personnel in St. Louis to tell them that he would not tolerate this kind of behavior. This type of behavior would not be tolerated unless of course your name was Heidenthal.

To say that a double standard existed at The Company was undoubtedly an understatement considering alleged offenses of a close relative to The Company's President. By comparison, my twist would be no more than "jaywalking." However, today The Company's President close relative is a high ranking official.

Finally, Sean was off the line, Mike's voice was very sullen, he stated the first hurdle was the legal entanglement in St. Louis, he would do what he could about our jobs.

Several weeks went by, it was the end of the year and travel was usually curtailed, I would tell Toni that I was calling on local wholesalers when in fact I was going to the library or to the movies. The time was sheer agony, I wondered what I would do if I had to go to jail in Missouri or if I were fired from The Company or if Toni ever found out. Finally, in the first week of December, I received a call from the attorney, all charges had been dropped. I could feel the tension leaving my body. That morning Mike Peterson called and informed me that Dan Dezenso wanted Sean and me to meet him in St. Louis that Friday. Mike said he didn't know what was going to transpire but to expect the worst. I called Sean in Cleveland and he thought we were going to be fired. I argued that the charges were dropped, therefore we were exonerated. We co-ordinated to arrive in St. Louis, since Sean's flight arrived first, he would come to my gate and meet me. Dan Dezenso wanted to see us one at a time, at the Airport we flipped a coin. Sean lost so he went to The Company headquarters first. We went to a restaurant where Sean got the telephone number. About an hour or so later Sean called, he had been fired and now Dan Dezenso and his mentor, my former Region Manager Phillip Jones, wanted to see me. I thought about just getting on the plane and not giving them the pleasure of firing me personally. Then I thought of taking my medicine like a man so I took a taxi to The Company Incorporated Headquarters. Sean met me in the lobby. He told me that he had called around The Company from the lobby and found out that Dave and Paul had also been fired today, reluctantly, from Davenport, Elliott, and Martin in Chicago at Hirsh's direction. I got my visitor's badge and took the elevator to the 4th floor, a few short steps to Dan Dezenso's office. Dan's secretary told me it would be just a moment before he was ready to see me, she asked the condemned if he would like a glass of water, I said "yes." A few moments later, I entered Dan's office.

Dan was in his early thirties, a guy whose rise in The Company was meteoric and unprecedented for someone not named Heidenthal. Dan was smiling as if he was about to pin a medal on me. I could sense his uneasiness about the situation, after all he was following orders from Hirsh. Standing with a stoic face was Phillip Jones. Dan was holding a folder which was obviously my personnel file, he was saying how much good stuff was inside and how I wouldn't have any problems finding new employment when Phillip Jones rudely interjected, "You're fired!" I wasn't sure if it was Jones' no frills personality or his fear that perhaps his young V.P. might not realize that his conversations could possibly be recorded. In any case, I asked about severance pay, to which Phillip replied, "There won't be any." I didn't bother to shake their hands, I said good-bye and left. Sean was waiting in the lobby. We took a taxi to the Airport and he was really upset. He really loved his work and The Company, also to make matters worse, his wife was six months pregnant. At the Airport, Sean wanted to call Mike Peterson at the Division Office, I thought, "it's over ... why bother." Sean and Mike spoke briefly, then Mike wanted to talk to me. He stated that he had been afraid that we were going to be fired, that he tried to help us keep our jobs until he was told to stay out of it. Our firing was an edict from Hirsh. Mike closed by saying he would make plans to have The Company car and equipment picked up. I shook Sean's hand and wished him the best, that day at the St. Louis Airport was the last time I saw Sean.

Monday morning, Mike Peterson called to say that on Tuesday, Victor and the Division Representative would come to Toledo to pick up the car and equipment. I asked Mike to have Victor call when he reached the neighborhood. I wanted to ensure that Toni was not home when they arrived. They arrived in a pickup truck. I had everything ready for them. They loaded the file cabinet and file boxes, the calculator, work organizer, typewriter, the car keys and the Lanier pocket tape recorder (minus the tapes!) I watched from the patio as they drove out of the driveway. As I watched I thought, "This is the first day of rest of my life, I better get busy!"

When Toni arrived home, she was surprised to find me home because The Company car was not parked outside. I explained that the car was at the dealer's for repairs. At dinner,

I laid the foundation for our move. I explained that I was very unhappy at The Company and that over the next week or so I would decide what to do. That weekend, I told Toni that I was going to resign from The Company and we would move to California. So that part of the charade was taken care of. I would resign on Monday to be effective January 1, 1985. Tony was due to take the Ohio Funeral Director's license test in early February, in the interim, I would pack our belongings for storage. January dragged by, I hadn't realized how much we had accumulated over the years, it took me days to pack everything. Finally, it was February. Toni passed the license test, of course, and Mayflower Storage Company came to collect our belongings. We packed Toni's car with our clothing and items we thought we would need, and on February 16, 1985, we said good-bye to Toledo, Ohio.

First stop was Chicago to spend a few days with my parents, and to have dental work by the new dentist in the family, my brother. Finally, we were off to the new world, it was winter, so we decided to take the Southern route. We drove south to Memphis, Tennessee; that evening at dinner I told Toni that in this very hotel I thought about nothing but her when I was on assignment here after we met. The next stop was New Orleans, we stayed an extra night so that we could take in the sights and the food. Then onward to Texas, a night in El Paso, and then on to San Antonio. Finally, it was a night in Phoenix, Arizona before heading into California. At the state border, we stopped to take pictures at the "Welcome to California" sign, we were all set to start our new life.

A friend of Toni's family was with the Board of Education and encouraged her to teach. I had numerous interviews but no offers, I was starting to feel desperate. Finally, through a friend of a friend and out of desperation, I took a job with a beer wholesalership and Toni started teaching.

With one car between us, we moved to one of those furnished temporary apartments that you could rent by the month and it happened to be a couple of blocks from Toni's school. We wanted to determine where we would live permanently before we had our belongings shipped out to California. Much to our dismay, the apartment came complete with roaches. Before our first month our car was victimized in the garage. My boss was a "dem, den and dose" type of guy who quickly came to fear my education and experience and Toni did not exactly take to teaching. After a particularly bad day, I came home to the news that Toni had quit her job. Without thinking I blurted out that she "was nothing but a liability." Toni asked me to leave. I grabbed a few belongings and went to a brother's apartment who had moved to California a year before.

I was so bitter about being fired after everything that I had been through. Undoubtedly, I was no longer the person Toni knew. I remembered what one of the District Managers once told me, "The Company will teach you how to hate!"

Rock Bottom

I had fallen from the Corporate Ladder, now I had fallen from grace. In such a short period of time, I had gone from eating in fine restaurants across the country to local fast food restaurants. From being married to a loving wife from a fine family to sleeping on my brother's couch. From driving a nice car to a dilapidated eyesore that hardly ran—my ego was taking a beating. I felt as though I had gone 15 rounds with an angry Muhammad Ali!

Growing up   12

I grew up and came of age in one of the toughest ghettos in the country, in a neighborhood called Woodlawn. It was a community of apartment buildings converted from single family apartments to multi-family. Several families would use one bathroom, rats and roaches were also principal tenants. Very few men headed households, my so-called friends would say that their fathers were in the military. If a father existed at all, the military was usually the state penitentiary. My parents were blue-collar workers, but determined that their children would be college graduates. My father, despite not having a degree, was industrious and successful. With no older brothers or cousins to champion my cause, I would walk to school through gangways (between apartment buildings) and backyards and through alleys to avoid the streets. Once inside the sanctuary of the apartment, there was no coming out, no store, no parks, only the companionship of television and books. My father worked, most of the children of the area were on ADC (Aid to Dependent Children). The style of dress for boys was blue jeans and brogans. Brogans were short boots with metal taps that covered the entire heel and toe. You learned early that in a fight you never go down, the crowd would kick the downed opponent in the head with those brogans. My mother was adamant that no matter how much we wanted to blend in, her children were going to dress as much like suburban white kids as possible.

Even if invited, my mother would not let us visit inside apartments for fear of the heroin that plagued my neighborhood. If there was one element that everyone in the neighborhood hated and mutually distrusted, it was the heroin addicts. During my years growing up, I witnessed a lot of hard-hitting guys with the hearts of lions fall prey to heroin. For the most part, there was a street code of ethics, sisters and mothers were usually hands-off. Even the winos in the neighborhood held a certain esteem, they were usually willing to work enough to afford a bottle of wine. However, the heroin junkie was without any regard, they would do anything, even suicidal things to get money for drugs. Once a neighbor's elbow was shattered. A junkie hid in a tree and when she walked underneath, he jumped on top of her knocking her to the ground. He did this just to get her purse. Junkies were also responsible for most of the burglaries whether anyone was home or not. We always had dogs in our house, big dogs, these were not pets, they were guard dogs. They could coexist with us for the most part. But their presence was more for security. And so it was through this backdrop of isolation and alienation that I became essentially a loner, as my father fostered, as I would appreciate when I was older—"self-reliant."

CHI-TOWN PART 1996

AN UPDATED PROFILE OF CHICAGO S BLACK STREET GANGS

LIFE STATEMENTS AND WALLS TAGGED WITH GRAFFITI USUALLY MARK GANG TERRITORY
RIGHT: 1968 PHOTO OF JEFF FORK, LEADER OF THE ALMIGHTY BLACK P-STONE NATION

The Evolution Of Chicago's Black Street Gangs

The New School

BY   SUDHIR   VENKATESH

THE SOURCE · APRIL 1996

The local gang was the Black Stone Rangers. In the sixties, it would evolve into the most notorious Black street gang in history. By high school, the Black Stone Rangers had evolved into one of the two largest gangs in Chicago, our rivals to the death were the Devil Disciples. During the sixties the leader of the Stones testified before the U.S. Congress in Washington, D.C. The government could not understand how a Black street gang could become so organized and violent.

Gang banging was losing its popularity and by my senior year of high school it had affected so many people and families adversely. Little boys who accidentally shot themselves playing with their older brothers' guns, friends who were shot and confined to a wheelchair for the rest of their lives, and then there were the ones that were killed or in jail. The gang leaders were now focusing on the members and factions that wanted out. There were shootings among the factions that wanted out and those that said you were gangbangers for life. By 1966 a lot of ex-Rangers had joined the Army in spite of the Vietnam war. To them even Vietnam was better than the streets of Chicago. Toward the end of my junior year, most of my faction, the Maniac Rangers, were in jail, the Army, or gone to the south to live with relatives to escape the street of Chicago. With all of my friends gone, I went from school to work at the store to home. In June 1968 I graduated, in September I headed for college in Ohio. I was leaving behind the world of hatred and mistrust, at least for a while.

Summary & Conclusion 13

Lessons I Have Learned

A great many young people have the same driving ambition that I did, I didn't have a sense of fear. I didn't have a sense that it could happen to me. I put all of the important things, family and life-style, behind me to drive toward this irrepressible goal.

Unfortunately, the society in the corporate world has it all setup where they are virtually dangling the brass ring in front of you. You never actually get the brass ring, and to get it, the few that seem to really get it, what price have they paid? Usually too much! Were they truly selected based on their intellect or brilliance or was it their lack of experience and resources that set them up for failure? They suffered what some call an illusion of inclusion.

Corporate employment was very similar to my experiences on the street with the gangs. Only they wore shirts and ties and carried briefcases, and the gangs wore tennis shoes, jeans and leather jackets. It's a jungle in the corporate world just as it is on the streets! You never know what corporate executives are planning and how you are going to fit into some of their bizarre plans. Your career is based on how you are going to react in these situations

Don't get me wrong. Ambition is good. However, there is sometimes too high a price to pay for ambition. In my case, I became embroiled in a situation that led to social isolation and a lack of access to resources. I had no significant social support or viable financial or human resources that I could utilize to help solve my dilemma. How could I handle it alone? I couldn't just quit my job and get another job the next day. I had to worry about job relocation or moving in order to get another job. So I lost my job, my wife, everything.

It is clear from my tragedy that an individual needs more than ambition. Employees in the corporate sector need the genuine support of the company's executives. These executives are restricted in their range of support due to the motion and direction of the corporation.

Liberal promotions are not the norm for organizations interested in maintaining control at all costs. They are often the ploy of organizations engaged in a bureaucratic game of manipulation, preying on the innocent and eager souls of the dedicated corporate worker.

Hopefully my tragedy will provide a kaleidoscope of awareness, a clear oasis in these putrid ashes. I would like people to realize that corporate success involves more than a diligent work ethic. It includes a carefully blended mixture of component parts operating in harmony—(1) the individual (2) the organization and (3) one's family.

Routine discrimination may be health hazard

By Marilyn Elias
USA TODAY

Repeated bouts of unfair treatment affect the races differently: Whites develop poor mental health, but blacks' physical and emotional health suffers, a new study suggests.

And the most health-damaging experiences apparently don't happen in major arenas — discrimination in the housing market, at work or school.

"It's the frequency of everyday' discrimination, chronic hassles, that's most strongly linked to health," says David Williams of University of Michigan's Institute for Social Research. Examples: poor service in public places, people treating you like you're not smart or acting afraid of you.

Williams' survey of 1,140 Detroit area adults looked at health measures such as how many days illness forced one to stay in bed, diagnoses of hypertension and symptoms of major emotional disorders.

For blacks, but not whites, the more "routine" experiences of unfairness reported the more sick days. Both major and "everyday" hassles predicted higher blood pressure for blacks.

Unfair treatment was linked to many mental health problems for whites — anxiety, panic attacks, phobias and depression — but only depression for blacks. Since blacks are far more likely to name skin color as the reason for unfair treatment, and color can't be changed, chronic stress may take a bigger toll on physical health, says Williams, and leave blacks more hopeless.

The findings show "our stereotypes may have some impact on other people's health," says Yale University psychologist Mahzarin Banaji. There evidence that "just about everybody has stereotypes, whether we think we ought to or not, whether we think we have them or not . . . These 'minor' events of stereotyping can add up, and the effects may be destructive for other people."

It seems only fitting that I should issue this warning in the 13th chapter. It's like the 13th floor of an office building, superstition excludes its existence. But the number 13 seems appropriate as an unlucky number for individuals who sell their personal integrity down the river. Ultimately, you don't win. It's a slow game of corporate suicide. The more of yourself you give up, the less of yourself you have left.

In my case, I lost everything. I even lost my soul. I have been imprisoned in a life of turmoil, guilt and unmitigated anguish since this whole experience began. My instincts were to expose The Company early. It was an imminent moral dilemma that I delayed too long. So long that eventually I was swallowed by the whale of corruption.

Corporate corruption is an insidious cancer. A cancer that eats at the core of the moral fabric of our country. A cancer that must be exposed over and over again. It's a negative sum game. There are no winners. Everyone loses! Greed, desire for personal wealth, clawing for advancement are the corner-stones of moral compromise. Yielding to these temptations is like selling your valueless soul to a litany of corporate demons. I hope my experience will be a harbinger for all who think "It could never happen to me!"

Experts Give Advice On Coping With Racism

Almost daily, news reports blare out the uncovering of yet another racial incident or attack. And more frequently millions of Black people in this country encounter an attitude, a remark or a situation that is spawned by racism.

So how can Black people, who inevitably will have to face some form of racism or discrimination at one point, deal with this evil fact of life? JET asked experts to share their advice on coping with racism.

The experts polled unanimously agree that racial attacks and comments must be dealt with, not ignored or internalized.

"They (people who encounter racism) need to respond to it," declares Silas Lee, III, a professor of sociology at Xavier University in New Orleans, LA. "It will not die; it will not go away. If we're waiting for the last racist to die, that will never happen."

The most effective way to handle a racial comment is to "deal with it straight up," says Dr. Robert Davis, director of institutional assessment and sociology professor at North Carolina A&T State University in Greensboro. "Let the person know that that comment or action is offensive."

For example, if a co-worker says something that offends you, let him or her know that it "was offensive to

▲ Silas Lee, III, a sociology professor at Xavier University in New Orleans, LA, says Blacks should, without a doubt, respond to racial attacks.

you and your race," Dr. Davis adds. Then let him or her know that "if further actions occur, you'll pass it on to a supervisor."

Experts also remind people to remember that some racial comments or attacks could actually be innocent.

"Sometimes people who commit (racial attacks) may not be aware," says Lee. He points to the fact that the workforce has changed drastically from a monolithic, White male environment to one with a diverse face. "All of the people are not able to communicate or relate to people of different backgrounds," Lee explains. "Make people aware of their transgressions."

Epilogue

During the boycott, The Organization's Leader referred to The Company programs targeted at the Black community as "Plantation Marketing" and "Token Gestures." What was being asked for was "ECONOMIC RECIPROCITY, not SOCIAL GENEROSITY," "PARITY not CHARITY," and "TRADE, not AID."

To the best of my knowledge, Black and other minorities are still underrepresented as The Company's Wholesalers.

Legacy

Walk the tightrope, maintain the balancing act—don't be militant, but remember you'll never be fully accepted and "watch your ass!"

REFERENCE BOOKS

Under the Influence, by Peter Hernon and Terry Ganey

The Wall Street Journal

ABOUT THE AUTHOR

Jim Hobson grew up during the turbulent sixties on Chicago's Southside Woodlawn area, birthplace of the Black Stone Rangers. The Black Street Gang that was so organized that it took on the MOB and captured the interest of lawmakers in Washington D.C.—The Civil Rights Era coupled with his streetwise experience with the gangs shaped his early consciousness of minorities plight in this country.

Jim currently lives in Southern California, he has served on the Board of the local Boys and Girls Club, and served on committee's for the Boy Scouts and The Muscular Dystrophy Association.

BOOK AVAILABLE THROUGH
Milligan Books, Inc.
An Imprint of Professional Business Consulting Service
And I Said No! $14.95

Order Form
Milligan Books, Inc.
1425 W. Manchester Ave., Suite C, Los Angeles, CA 90047
(323) 750-3592

Name_____ Date _____

Address_____

City_____ State____ Zip _____

Day Telephone _____

Evening Telephone_____

Book Title_____

Number of books ordered___ Total ....$ _____

Sales Taxes (CA add 8.25%).....................$ _____

Shipping & Handling $4.90 for one book ..$ _____

Add $1.00 for each additional book ....$ _____

Total Amount Due...............................$ _____

☐ Check ☐ Money Order ☐ Other Cards _____

☐ V isa ☐ MasterCard Expiration Date_____

Credit Card No. _____

Driver License No. _____

State ID Card No. _____

Make check payable to Milligan Books, Inc.

_____   _____
Signature   Date